THE BRIDPORT PRIZE 2020

POETRY, SHORT STORIES AND FLASH FICTION

JUDGES
Mimi Khalvati • Poetry
Nell Leyshon • Short Stories and Flash Fiction

First published in 2020 by Redcliffe Press Ltd
81g Pembroke Road, Bristol BS8 3EA
e: info@redcliffepress.co.uk
www.redcliffepress.co.uk

Follow us on Twitter @RedcliffePress
© the contributors

Follow The Bridport Prize:
Follow us on Twitter @BridportPrize

www.bridportprize.org.uk
www.facebook.com/bridportprize

ISBN 978-1-911408-74-1

British Library Cataloguing-in-Publication Data
A catalogue record for this book is available from the British Library
All rights reserved. Except for the purpose of review, no part of this book may be reproduced, stored in a retrieval system, or transmitted, in any form or by any means, electronic, mechanical, photocopying, recording or otherwise, without the prior permission of the publishers.

Typeset in 10.5pt Times

Typeset by Addison Print Ltd, Northampton
Printed by Hobbs the Printers Ltd, Totton

Contents

Poetry Report Mimi Khalvati	5
Short Story Report Nell Leyshon	7
Flash Fiction Report Nell Leyshon	10
Low Tide Michael Lavers	13
After Blue Luke Allan	15
Dunnock in the Bird Bath Rowland Molony	16
Kurt Cobain Receives a Fax from Courtney Love Jonathan Edwards	17
Vee Oit John Freeman	18
Travelling for the Hell of it Karen Green	20
Waty Watson, Railroad Engineer Justin Hunt	21
Jimmy Beverley Nadin	22
The Chinese Typewriter John O'Donoghue	23
FAGS AND WORK Mario Petrucci	25
In the Museum of Childhood Maya C. Popa	27
Naked Julie-ann Rowell	29
Unfinished Knitting Di Slaney	30
Oh, Hululu Debra Waters	31
Fight, Flight, Freeze, Comply, Film (FFFCF) Cara George	42
What the Deal is Dafydd Mills Daniel	47
She Came to Stay Erika Banerji	58
The Box Alistair Daniel	70
The Note Alex Dawes	75
That Kind of Girl Elizabeth Fremantle	87
Call Rachael Fulton	90
The Graduation Sarah Harte	98
Sandals Nida Manzoor	103
Milk Laurane Marchive	106
Loving Sam David Alexander McFarland	120
The Judgment of Paris Rachel Sloan	130
Mum Died Rowena Warwick	134
Tamed Gaynor Jones	135
Fabulous at Fifty Olga Moroni	136
Bring and Buy Lydia Clark	137
The one about the hole in the front garden Nicola Shilcock	138
On a Supermarket Toilet Floor Richard Smith	139
Biographies	140

MIMI KHALVATI

Poetry Report

It has been a real pleasure to be the judge this year for the Bridport Poetry Competition. Despite the pandemic, there was a high number of entries and I am full of admiration for those of you who have managed to continue writing, keeping poetry alive at a time when it is sorely needed. During lockdown, while I was shielding, the shortlisted poems I read kept me company with their living presences. I am deeply grateful to the authors for bringing the richness of their experiences into my orbit and sharing them with me. I am grateful too to the discerning shortlisting panel who sent me the poems, all of which were worthy, none of which I could pass over, though of course this made my job more difficult. So many of the poems fulfilled my expectations. But they subverted them too. There were few poems about coronavirus, but a surprising number of formal poems and a wealth of character studies, as though lockdown had invited a host of players into an empty arena to fill it with their voices.

The hardest part of the judging process was choosing the Highly Commended poems but here they are, retaining their shine after many shufflings, in no particular order. The Highly Commended poems are:

'Vee Oit': I was immediately drawn to this poem by the charm of the title and the play on languages, spellings and pronounciations. I loved it for its candour, modesty, and the smooth shifts in register from the anecdotal to the lyrical.

'The Chinese Typewriter': The conceit of this sestina, drawing from the epigraph its six repetends, each imbued with the necessary emotional freight, is inspired and results in a bold and fresh take on familiar themes.

'Jimmy' is full of empathy without sentimentality and evokes convincingly the reality of a psychiatric ward. The intricate form enacts the protagonist's stance, like a boxer on his toes – close-fisted, balled up, warding off attack.

'In the Museum of Childhood' is unusual in moving fearlessly between concrete images and abstractions, weaving its meditative power. The final statement moves me every time I read it, leaving me with a helpless silence.

'FAGS AND WORK': Upon the modulated syntax of this poem hangs a slowly revolving series of images, marvellously detailed, of the speaker's father. The sense of gratitude is profound in this elegy and paean for him and his labours.

'Naked': Despite its difficult subject matter, this poem is written in a very relaxed vernacular, convincing in its familiarity with FND and the explosive daily life in the centre. A poem that poignantly enhances our understanding.

'Waty Watson, Railroad Engineer' is an energetic and triumphal portrait, filmic in the way scenes reel past. There is no main verb in the whole poem – as if its absence stands for Waty Watson himself, so desperately active in life.

'Travelling for the Hell of it' is a wonderfully quirky take on ageing, whose ghastly details are here observed almost lovingly with forensic exactitude. I love the deadpan tone, the mordant, mischievous wit, the mock horror ending.

'Kurt Cobain Receives a Fax from Courtney Love, Royal Hotel, Amsterdam, November 1991': At first I felt daunted by so much 'data', but then seduced by the expert handling of the narrative with its retro aura that led unexpectedly to such an endearing conclusion.

'Unfinished Knitting': I was delighted to come upon a poem that takes the aesthetic risks commonly associated with 'femininity' and overcomes them by sheer musicality, technical facility, knitting vocabulary, and pure lyric pleasure.

Finally, here are my three prize winners. Third prize is won by 'Dunnock in the Bird Bath'. This poem positively leaps off the page in a flurry of bird-language and activity. More experimental than the others, but not arbitrarily so, this is a delicious poem to love, celebrate and spontaneously applaud.

My second prize winner is 'After Blue'. I was immediately drawn to this poem by the playfulness of the opening, its confident repetitions, then drawn in further by the voice confiding its intimacies, then still further down to its aching tenderness for a beloved. This is a mysteriously beautiful poem which spirals, as if in a vortex, down to the core and alights there.

First Prize goes to 'Low Tide', a gorgeous lyric which comes in sixes: six-line verses covering six days of a six-year-old. Its formal aspects, finely judged rhymes, heterometric lines, graceful syntax, convey the multiplicity of sealife washed up onshore, which in turn reflects the life-cycle of childhood itself, now here, now gone forever. A poem of great sensitivity and strength.

My warmest congratulations to the prize winners, to all those highly commended and on the shortlist, and many thanks to the organisers for inviting me to judge this year's competition. It has been a hugely rewarding experience.

NELL LEYSHON

Short Story Report

To write a successful short story is a real challenge and harder than people think. There are no rules, but some things help: a clear point of view, a tight focus, an idea of how time passes within the narrative. It is like juggling as you throw a certain number of elements up into the air then you have to land them carefully and in order.

The quality of the work I read was extraordinarily high and judging them felt like a huge responsibility. I was looking for a voice, a writer who had something to say, but I found so many voices. There is nothing quite like the thrill of finding fresh phrasing and imagery. There are ten highly commended stories.

'The Box' is completely original. It withholds information brilliantly and forces you to read on to find out what it is in the box and what it means. The story explores gender in a unique way and the ending was a real surprise. 'Sandals' takes the well-told theme of arranged marriage and subverts it, finding an original voice which is dark and full of humour. The way the character's real self is revealed shows a strong and defensive interior world. *Okay, so yeah I had a breakdown, which is why I'm here.* I was really gripped reading 'Milk'; the texts within the story really work (not that easy to pull off) and it has real confidence. It made me think about why we continue to read a story, why we need to get to the end.

'The Note' is about writing and feedback, truth and delusion. It's a witty, very well-crafted story which never reveals the contents of the note (I loved that), yet creates a whole believable world with fully drawn characters. 'Loving Sam' is also well-crafted and beautifully written, full of detail and great dialogue. *She winnowed our wardrobe to the essentials, two pairs of good shoes for me – one brown, one black, five for her – which was one more than she had allowed before.* The story of the two Sams – the car and the stepdad – is very moving.

'The Graduation' is also full of great dialogue which adds to its huge energy. It's short yet says so much and is full of wisdom and confidence. *She wonders what all the striving is about, when everyone is on a collision course with death.* I'd love to read a novel by this writer – the characters and settings are so vivid and have real depth.

Writing in the second person is hard to do well and can be jarring, yet there were two stories I admired which did exactly that. The writing of 'The Judgment of Paris' is confident and assured, right from the first paragraph. There is a strong voice here and some fantastic imagery: *Your politesse has grown over your mouth like tree bark and you're trapped inside.* 'Call' is a very different story. A deep emotional story of two sisters, it uses original phrasing and language. The narrator fantasises about bludgeoning her sister with the old tennis racquet and says, *She bangs things up and down on the surfaces, drags storms behind her.*

'She Came to Stay' is a wonderful story of a recently arrived immigrant family from Kolkata and their lodger who has an effect on the family. It is a great piece of story-telling and is both gripping and elegantly written with a clarity and simplicity of sentence: *The pavements on Maple Drive were scattered with the first fall of yellow leaves.* The final highly commended story, 'That Kind of Girl', is an experimental piece told in one sentence and begins and ends with the phrase *that kind of girl*. It is beautifully written and emotionally disturbing to read. An exploration of consent and early sexual experiences, it's a great marriage of content and form.

The story I chose for third prize, 'What The Deal Is', is a highly musical piece with a truly original voice. Each paragraph is one sentence and the layout and punctuation are original and add to the musicality. It tells us how human beings are treated, how human society is ordered. It felt like a microcosm of the world, especially when you realise at the end of the story that the owner *never once took no black guy there*. It is at once a horrible mirror on the world and a brilliant piece of writing which contains *all kinds of cruel imaginings.*

The second prize, 'Fight, Flight, Freeze, Comply, Film (FFFCF)', is also a wholly original piece. A story of how *all the birds flew straight up* and disappeared, it felt right for this time of pandemic and climate crisis. It tells of a dystopian world with no birds, yet it is written with such incredible confidence, imagery and humour. It is completely vital. At times you laugh: *Cat on cat crime went up*. At other times you want to cry at the thought of a world without birds, particularly after we heard them sing so loudly during quarantine.

'Oh, Hululu' is the winning story. It is both an original voice and a perfect piece of writing. It tells of a woman who has a crush for six months and is an anti-love love story. It has acerbic wit and every line feels crafted and necessary. It is written in the second person, yet its distancing feels true to the story: the coldness with which the narrator views herself is glorious and is often explained further in italics within brackets: *'I'm a terrible mother.'* (*You're not, you're fierce. Coarse-tongued as a pirate but every inch is love.*) There are so many passages of superb writing: *Your longing leaves a snail trail, an invisible viscid liquid on the bedding, the steering wheel, the rim of your wine glass.*

Superb work, all. What a privilege to read your words. Thank you.

NELL LEYSHON

Flash Fiction Report

It's a great lesson to see how much can be expressed in 250 words or less, and reminds us economy can be a wonderful thing as it allows a story to blossom in the reader's mind. I read stories where whole worlds were created, stories which illuminated part of history, stories which made serious points, and stories which were light and fun.

There are three highly commended stories: 'The one about the hole in the front garden' filled me with warmth and wonder and sent me back into my own childhood memories. The colours are beautiful and the last image of the children circling the hole sucking on orange ice pops is so vivid and real.

'Bring and Buy' is confident and draws you in to a chain of events which fill you with horror. The stakes get higher and higher and we are left devastated, questioning the everyday exchange of money for goods. 'On a Supermarket Toilet Floor' plays with one rule of short fiction extremely well, proving that rules are there to be broken. It breaks the point of view and switches from the girl who has harmed herself to the man who saves her. It is brave and bold and incredibly successful.

The worst thing about reading these stories was having to decide on a top three. It becomes about what works, but also what touches you as a reader, what you respond to. The third prize is for 'Fabulous at Fifty' which gets better the more you read it. It is about an outsider, about the assumptions people make when they meet you, and about the massive backstory some people carry. The loaded line, *I left what I knew behind* reveals so little and yet so much. The story is full of controlled anger.

The second prize, 'Tamed', grows in importance as you re-read it. The first part is a young woman in control; as the story enters the second half, we see that her story about *her wild thing* has been stolen from her. She has moved from being the subject of the story to the object. In the telling of the story, it feels as though the narrator takes the power back: it is hers to tell again.

I never doubted which story would get the first prize. 'Mum Died' is odd, original, and you can't quite pin it down. What does it mean to die over and over? She *died several times in Dad's Ford Anglia when he was teaching her to drive.* And again: *She died in those shoes which were the wrong colour on my wedding day.* And again: *She died with the arrival of each grandchild.*

There is a whole life in here and we see the highs and lows as the list grows of the times her mum died. And then the story transitions at the end from past tense to present tense and concludes with extraordinary elegance. *But more recently she has used it all up, her skill in dying.* I have read it so many times and it keeps on growing and blossoming in my mind.

POETRY FIRST PRIZE

MICHAEL LAVERS

Low Tide

      For six straight days
my bored suburban six-year-old has floated
      in a sun-stroked daze,
   in love with all the lavish frills he's found,
gobbets of flesh the heat has bloated,
      shriveled, blanched, and browned—

      not nereids
sporting in waves, not Venus on her shell,
      but silky worms, dried squids,
   weird scraps of lace the tiderocks hooked and tore,
the cast-off underthings of hell
      strewn on the sandy floor.

      Spent seastars cool
their nether-parts in mud. An eel delves
      through eels. Jellies pool
   and lift their skirts for an anemone
as startled clams unsquirt themselves,
      and urchins shine like money.

      Soon my son's rich
in captives: cockles and chitons stewed in scum,
      that same concoction which
   conspired with a primal sky
and made a sea's unconscious sum
      divide and multiply.

      At dusk, downshore,
we take his pail of temporary pets
      and, kneeling, start to pour
   them out, cucumbers, crablings, snails, this glut

of shells and gauzy silhouettes
>> he wants forever. But

>> we're driving home.
How long could any forms this frail last?
>> We rinse our hands in foam
> and walk back through the woods where shadows grow,
and mayflies flare and dive, who just
>> last night were embryo.

POETRY SECOND PRIZE

LUKE ALLAN

After Blue

I like that feeling of almost not reaching the sea
but turning back from turning back
and continuing outwards anyway despite
the emptiness. Of planes I thought were stars
turning out to be planes, then turning out to
be stars. Some people don't exist anymore,
that's weird. And some planes act like they're
bigger deals than they are. I can touch your eyebrow
with my nose and that too is part of the twenty-first
century. Whatever else it is, a plane is a box
full of people who could have been our friends,
of people breathing air fresher than this
rubbish seaside wind. I thought becoming a husband
would rubberstamp me as a man, but I sing
christmas carols in the shower in the dark and I
don't know. Or I brush my teeth in the mirror
in the afterglow of sex and think maybe my face is
actually sort of beautiful? Like when we could hear
that waterfall from the roadside, but couldn't agree
which direction it was coming from. It's impossible
to know where your beauty is. It hits you in
the evening, then disappears overnight. I do the dishes
while you sleep, as quietly as possible, but it's
not enough. Or I brush my hair with your hairbrush
while you're awake, and it helps me to imagine
your loneliness. And when your head calls my name
from the living room, I come to it.

POETRY THIRD PRIZE

ROWLAND MOLONY

Dunnock in the Bird Bath

head up   anyone see me?
    no   head down then   squiddle   flutter   spritz
              wateringup feathers   head-dunk   flicker & splash
   head up   look about   anyone?   no   fizzup & lather

anyone about?   no   skidaddle in again then   shuffle the spray
             flitter the feathers   look out 360°   no one about?
     back down head down arse up belly down
            shuffle the feathers   spraddle & sprinkle & fling

 tremble the feathers   vibrate the spray
     shower all up & over & in & down & under & up-the-featherage
anyone see me?   no   anyone?   no

still nobody   one more then   dunk-in-under   last plug-in
    to a fizz of voltage
        whirr the enginewings in the sunlight

charged up

JONATHAN EDWARDS

Kurt Cobain Receives a Fax from Courtney Love, Royal Hotel, Amsterdam, November 1991

The fax will later be found folded in the inside pocket of a jacket,
in a wardrobe at the house he will die in. It will be auctioned
for $50,000 in a lot which includes the jacket, a Nirvana-logo'd

frisbee, a toothbrush he may once have used. It will be quoted
in a biography it will take the writer four years and four hundred
interviews to complete, and the quotation will be disputed by Love herself,

or the legal representatives of Love herself. There are three years
between the fax being sent and Cobain's death – three years, in which
he gets married, becomes a father, sells four million records

and consumes so much heroin, Seattle fills with dealers
who will not sell to him. None of that matters to the man
who stands here, now, the business centre of a five-star hotel

in Amsterdam, two in the morning, waiting for a fax from the woman
he loves. She's on tour with her band in Chicago, or – he forgets –
Boston, and he's hunched here at the fax machine, waiting for it to print so,

so slowly. Twenty years before smart phones, texts,
Tinder, and the most famous musicians on the planet are in different
time zones, wooing each other by fax. Now his eyes scan down

past the explicit sexual reference, the scatological puns, the allusions
to the lyrics of obscure guitar bands, the straightforward gobbledygook, to
what he wants to see: the way she signs off. There are holes in his sweater,

track marks in his arms, the latest estimate puts his personal fortune
at three million dollars, and anyone passing the glass wall
of the business centre now, walking along this plush, plush carpet,

may look in and see this: a man alone in a room,
tearing from a machine a fax. Then punching the air, then hugging it
to his chest, then beginning slowly, shyly, shufflingly to dance.

JOHN FREEMAN

Vee Oit

When I think of people at a distance
from any centre, I remember Mayshtree –
that's a rough English approximation
of her Bavarian name, perhaps in German
Mäshtri, but I never saw it written.
Vee oit, she asked me, which the lad my age
translated, *wie alt*, she wants to know how old.
I was sixteen and certainly looked younger.
She was bent and her face was half concealed
by the scarf she could barely see out under,
but neither her age nor her heavy clothing
interfered with how she used a scythe
to mow the wheat in that strip of the field
where the German boy and I were helping.
I learned to tell wheat from rye, oats and barley
by their German names before I could have said
what sort of grass the English words referred to,
though I'd read about the bearded barley,
seen ears of wheat on packets of brown flour,
and heard a phrase about sowing wild oats.
Mäshtri had lived her life in this small village.
She'd moved with the times, used fertilizer
with too heavy a hand. Günter pointed.
You see that strip over there on the slope
where the corn is all flattened, where it's lying?
That's hers. That other strip? That's hers as well.
I was invited to her house, glanced over
the half door opposite where we had entered
and saw a tranquil cow stretched out on straw.
I peered up the chimney as invited
and glimpsed blue sky above the hanging ham.
I was the sole outsider in the village,
but a couple from Bremen passed through once
and told me that they couldn't understand

the dialect any better than I could.
Mäshtri wanted to know where I was from.
London, I answered, as if that explained it.
She looked blank. Günter gestured towards the hill.
Over there, he said. Further than Nuremberg.

KAREN GREEN

Travelling for the Hell of it

In addition she has been noticing how the edges
of the teeth, especially the molars, have become
sharp, like old shells worn down by many tides,
and running the tip of the tongue around the mouth

she half expects a trickle of blood to stain her handkerchief.
The skin of the palm of the hand is now more sensitized
to disagreeable surfaces – the greasy metal handrail
at the airport descending to the claustrophobic gate.

The muscles of the mouth no longer hold in beverages,
water, wine or tea. She has to make a conscious effort
to raise up the corners of her mouth or else it droops
in a permanent charade of melancholy.

And then there's the gag reflex, seemingly more frequent
and more sensitive to agents put in the mouth,
those multisized and maniform tablets and capsules
that personal biochemistry requires on a daily basis.

Now coming down the stairs she needs to concentrate
harder than ever not to lose her footing;
instead of her whole past life reeling before her eyes
she sees the scenario from this point fast-forward.

At the mountain teashop, Fidazhof, across the road
to the white church, she sips her rum and coffee;
the unseen Swiss speak Romansch, their incognito voices
cold water babbling over gravel at the bottom of a brook.

On the last morning she packs her black metal case
with its armoury of ribs. She has no idea
which random objects stay in the flat and what
she should carry home. Leaving is always purgatory.

JUSTIN HUNT

Waty Watson, Railroad Engineer

who, after several attempts, finally did himself in,

                                            but not before
he rode his horse on the sidewalk and pummeled
the marshal who tried to arrest him, which landed
him in the county jail down in Wellington for a year
and cured him of drink, though it didn't put ground
under his legs, or stop him from buzzing his neighbors
in a rented Cessna—like the time he yelled down
at Edgar Mathes, yanked up the plane's nose and stalled,
then dove in steep flirtation with his demise—

                                            and not before
he quit paying his water bills, got cut off by the town
and trudged down to Meils Hardware, came back
with three sticks of dynamite, determined to drill and blast
his own well, which shattered the windows next door
and across the alley, made a rain of shards that sharpened
the lie he told himself—that no one liked him.

Wild old Waty, who mounted silver air horns
to his Model-A truck and trumpeted our dusty streets,
railroader's cap askew, star-dazed even by day,
bugling for answers we couldn't give him—a word
or sign, just one that might have scattered the storm
gathering behind his eyes, the fury that broke

                                        that August morning
as he hammered down the rails over by Milton,
alone at the throttle of a Missouri Pacific diesel,
his engineer days almost done—one last run,
sixty miles per hour on tracks posted twenty, locomotive
throating, wheels screeching into wind

                everything he'd wanted to say but couldn't.

BEVERLEY NADIN

Jimmy

Found in a skate park, brought here for your safety
    in a police van
you're restless as a fledgling for the sky,
laces trailing, joggers sliding down,
skinny ribs in the gaping hospital gown
    and one black eye.

You pace the ward, resisting sleep all night,
    voice cracked with the strain
of venting pressured streams of frantic thought.
Jimmy, what's the storm you can't keep in?
Shivering on the smokers' bench in the rain
    until first light.

You spring up, showering tablets on the nurse,
    certain he's some guy
you jostled for a fight and came off worse.
Why they're signing forms to make you stay
and why they locked your pocket knife away,
    you're at a loss.

Even as your balled fist smashes clean
    through the consultant's door,
it's you that's more astonished than anyone,
big-eyed, suddenly sorry, but what for
is beyond you, glass in slivers on the floor,
    the anger gone.

To find some peace of mind would be enough.
    Jimmy, forcing a toke
on a stub too dead to burn, it sets you off,
croaking through catarrh in a coughing attack,
the last kid from your class not dead from smack
    or jailed for life.

JOHN O'DONOGHUE

The Chinese Typewriter

Even in this aged condition, though, the machine still bore the signature of what had clearly been a deeply personal relationship between the device, the typist who used it, and the man in whose employ this typist worked... the first shimmer of characters came to light: emigrant, far away, urgent... and a second constellation came into view: longing, hardship, dream. Not unexpectedly, one of the crispest characters on the tray bed was *hong*, Y.C. Hong's surname. Traces of the life this machine had lived still lingered, even decades later.

The Chinese Typewriter: A History, pp. 163 – 164, Thomas S. Mullaney, MIT Press, 2017

In America they call me 'emigrant'.
This continent's a different world, far away
From China, where I send my letters marked *urgent*,
As if by this they'd fly, my tales of longing
Concealed in characters I encrypt. Hardship
Can have no place in the American Dream.

To mechanise calligraphy. A new dream
In this new world, where each emigrant
Must set aside themselves, start anew, hardship
Relegated to the past, the far away.
But I'm not sure any more of belonging,
A character in a machine, insurgent

Against all that is fast, inhuman, urgent.
I am like the butterfly in Chang Chou's dream,
Estranged somehow from myself, longing, longing
To know if I'm man or merely emigrant.
Cherry blossom falls so very far away
And every life I know must reckon hardship

John O'Donoghue

For itself, though I had not thought the hoared ship
That brought me here over the rolling urgent
Waves would find a teeming world so far away.
It feels as if I've strayed into some bad dream
Where I am now the reverse, the 'emigrant',
Of all who look at me askance. A longing

Takes hold of my heart, a deep, painful longing
To return to Shenyang, but back home hardship
Too awaits me, and so like the emigrant
I've become I adjust. Perhaps this urgent
Ache will dull with time, yet at night I still dream
Of streets and squares I knew, lost and far away.

Sometimes when my master sees the far away
Look in my eyes, I can sense his own longing
For home. It shimmers like a luminous dream
Between us then, and I forget my hardship.
But then he snaps out of it, tells me urgent
Letters need my attention, one emigrant

To another, and far away like hardship
Is banished. But longing remains, as urgent
As breath, as the dream of every emigrant.

MARIO PETRUCCI

FAGS AND WORK

I wondered what it was – this *work*
        that because of us you had to do – work
                that fumbled you through the house so early

that hours later when I woke I'd swear
        the dark had used your voice to swap curses
                with the light half-dreamt at my window

and here and there through noons of ludo
        and hangman or making matchbox radios
                came the thought: what designs had work

upon a frame so wide we'd use your shadow
        each summer for shade? what steep weight
                work must have had – to slow you up our street

with its pall so upon you as to make brothers
        pause mid-tackle at the dad-shaped dust
                that puffed up the hill: a figure whose

one-knee-before-the-other walk seemed never
        to get any nearer – and being sometimes so
                late you'd no time to wash you would just

lower yourself to table as you were – one
        hand planted firm and elbow bent below
                its roll of sleeve as though that arm were

crane to the payload of a day-worth self
        without whose patina of labour men like you
                could not exist nor dare to seat themselves

at table where always was set stout cooking
        (for men who pour such sweat wither on salads)
                while we fingered in your shirt the yellowed

Mario Petrucci

bullet-hole a fag had made or traced Martian
>canals half-mucked into your lifelines until
>>that slurp of spooning so slowed you could

strike a match and call on us one by one to give
>account of idle days in which always we were
>>guilty till proven innocent — Ah I've worked

unbroken since – and not alone with ink and paper
>for even I among brothers squatted with you too
>>young between barrows and shovels or served

to smear soft cheeses of grout into your squared
>cracks of tiles though once – when no one looked
>>or cared to look – I hung fire so you could light up

and take the drag that told me what a son you had

MAYA C. POPA

In the Museum of Childhood

It's yours I remember,
and Larkin's, who called his
a forgotten boredom.

How it might just as well
have never happened,
though it did once,

it happened once, to you,
in a house with a moat
and no heating,

twin voices boiling over
in the kitchen below.
You'd survive it all,

which is to say, forsake,
those days turning in you
like a pinwheel still,

that base from which
language understands
its failure. There was time

to be apart and still a part
of something human
before the usual forfeiture

of green to cities, days blunted
by the millstone of duty.
Now the hours blink back

with the eyes of roadside
animals, and the disks shrink
with not enough of anything

worth keeping. You could weep
for all you did not know then
was a blessing, the voices

hurt and angry but living
nonetheless, the highway throbbing
with its dreamed-of passages.

The museum makes converts
out of visitors—I lug youth's
icons inside me and believe:

we bear that loss we caused
by our arriving. We were never
loved by anything

the way tomorrow loved us then.

JULIE-ANN ROWELL

Naked

He's in the garden again, disrobed,
just his boxers, though they've told him
keep covered up, it's the rules:
no PJs in the common rooms, outside,
no dressing gowns or bare torsos.
He never takes it in and we're not sure why,
the rest of us internees, our problems
worn like shields and yet we're defenceless.
His room is opposite mine,
during the night he'd wander inside
looking for something elusive. I'd scream
and he'd scoot like a rabbit.
He can't sit still, he's asleep
or on the go, a roll-up, a can of Vimto
though he'd prefer alcohol – we're dry
here (God knows I'd love a glass of wine).
It was late when he arrived and dived
in and out of our rooms to squeals and shouts –
women in various states of undress,
a strange man on the rove. Our
spasms and jerks, our tics and faints
gathering apace, enough energy
to lift the roof off our little centre
for FND, that no one's ever heard of.
Lucy, next door, complains until
he is tailed by a nurse twenty-four
hours – he's only here a day or two
which turns into weeks. Not FND – he
was attacked by his ex with a brick,
and now he wanders constantly, searching
for answers. This is no place for
finding those, we're lost in
clouds and mists, the young girl
fitting in the corridor, and me with the boy
leaning heavily on his walking stick.

FND: Functional Neurological Disorder

DI SLANEY

Unfinished Knitting

She held patterns in her feet
and in her fingers, eight soft strands
of daisy, gorse, thrift, pine and peat.
She danced patterns with her feet
in reels on Skye, Iona, Barra, Mull, Tiree
and Fair Isle; moorit, mooskit, eesit in her hands.
She made patterns with her feet
and with her fingers, eight warm strands

carried right to left to craft Norwegian stars
and shore the heart in his broad chest.
Advance, retire, loop and cast – the yarn
rose left and right to trap the stars
and steek the gaps. She heard the far
off birds on islands in the west,
calls carried right to left to lull the stars
and soothe the heart in his broad chest

with patterns growing from her fingers,
patterns slowing down her blood.
Orris in her mixed pourri will linger
in all the patterns flowing from her fingers,
tangled in eight coloured threads to bring
her blooming petalled bruises from the bud
and patterns slowing from her fingers,
patterns growing in her blood.

SHORT STORY FIRST PRIZE

DEBRA WATERS

Oh, Hululu

Month one

You meet him in an unseasonably warm October. You're on the same course. You're wearing jeans, a red jumper, flat boots; it's the last time you dress down. You like his tree-like height and his hair – was it auburn, once? Blonde? You're not sure why but this charms you.

College is in a dirty-aired part of town. Your classroom faces an air-conditioning unit that doubles as a pigeon graveyard. You're nervous and chatty; he's quiet. You find yourself wishing he'd talk more so you'd have a reason to look his way. At break he's slyly flirtatious, reminds you of a bad ending boyfriend. Still, you're drawn to his clear eyes – their halo effect – and how, when he expresses himself, he unfurls his long fingers and bares his deep-lined palms like a magician unveiling a trick. Ta da!

Afterwards, your group heads to a bar where the servers are too cool to smile. A wolfhound called Trouble lives there. The women buy bottles of wine to share, the men pints. You tell him you're married to G, have a young son, S. He's single, no kids. He travels, you're scared of flying.

When you realise you're at least a decade older than him you head to the toilet and reapply your make-up. At the bar you down Sauvignon until the booze takes over your tongue. When his answers turn circumspect, equivocal, you feel like a nosy aunt – you may as well ask him what he wants to be when he grows up – but he doesn't move seats.

He's unlike anyone you know, as familiar as a childhood friend. The biscuit-coloured mole on his arm acts like a homing device – you stay by the mole until closing time. On the way out, you stroke the dog; Trouble licks your hand.

At the station your friend E asks you what you think of him.

'I'm not sure.' *(You're sure.)*

At home G asks, 'Are there any men on the course?'

'No,' you say, because he's referring to threats.

Your feelings for G are soft, pedestrian, integral. Keep you steady as you go. You like your life, your terrace with its fitful plumbing, your white dog and medium-sized family car. You're comfortably numb, think this is a good thing. G thinks not.

'You know that song's about tranquilizers?'

'Of course.' *(And a tranquilized life is a painless one.)*

The following week you sit behind him at a lecture. Your mind wanders; there's a whirlpool swirl of hair on his crown, there are creases in his neck you'd like to iron with your thumb, there's space between his hair and shirt you wish to Eskimo-kiss.

Later, your group heads to the bar; you're on a shared journey to find the right words, think when they come you'll find meaning. You walk beside him, feel an uncanny calm, a happy-go-lucky clarity. You've replaced your mumsy underwear with a cerise two-piece – its brightness goaded you – and the peeping lace catches his eye.

(Remove your wife coat, slip out of your mother dress. Go on, tell him who you used to be, how you learned to dive in Thailand, how placid sharks seem underwater.)

You tell him you walked the Tongariro Crossing, saw several landscapes in an afternoon. He talks about living abroad and you wear your listening-attentively-look but really you're watching his fingers and willing them to your waist.

'Where to next?' he asks.

'Um, Pompeii?' you say.

(You were a Roman empress once; your name was Lascivious Maxima. You had many sons by many lovers.)

'Good choice. Have you been to Japan?'

'No. Shall we go?'

It's a stupid answer. He smiles, humours you. He travels alone, swears he doesn't get lonely. You don't believe him, can't shake the feeling he needs you. When you hug goodbye you're warmed by the heat of his skin but you also sense a hollow in his chest; it makes you want to move in, set up home *(but no cats, he's allergic)*. You stay in his hold longer than you should, your cheek against his tango-style, and when you pull back his neck's flushed to a blush.

(You're crushing it.)

'There's something about him,' you tell E. It's said to raise a smile, it's lust parked in a cul-de-sac.

'You must be ovulating,' she says.

'What makes you think that?'

'I read it makes women our age horny. Last chance saloon.'

'I've got G for that.'

'Right you are.'

Month two

You're on a train home, watching merging streaks of bricks. You sat next to him today; at one point your knees touched.

You arrive home fluey, air-kiss G and head for bed. 'I'm coming down with something, I'll sleep in the spare room,' you say. It's peaceful in there, like someone died a happy death. That night he texts, nothing flirty. You reply, something friendly. In the early hours you have a nightmare; you're at opposite ends of a crowded train carriage. You call out but he ignores you, makes you a ghost in your own dream.

You wake up red-faced, feverish, hungry.

As days pass, your mind – normally crammed with schoolbooks and whitewashes and grocery dashes – fills with him. It's your imagination but it's palpable. When you cook he's a hologram leaning against the fridge describing his day *(you reply wisely, hilariously, ha-ha)*; when you shower he's pressed against your back, his hand cupping the baby-made curve of your stomach; when G stays up to shout at 'Question Time' you lie in bed reciting his name like a spell.

You rationalise; you're overworked and need a distraction. You're rarely alone, it's his aloneness you crave. You're tired and nebulously depressed and that's why you see his initials in car number plates and LBD *(libido)*, CRH *(crush)*, LSS *(loss)*. The time's always 11:11, 15:15, 00:00 but you've read about this, it's the Baader-Meinhof effect, the frequency illusion. Nothing a good night's sleep can't solve.

You can't sleep.

'You're restless,' says G. 'Are you taking care of yourself?'

G thinks no one can take better care of you than him. *(That doesn't stop you thinking there's someone else up to the job.)*

'Sure, love.'

When you next meet your classmates for drinks Trouble's hiding behind the bar. You stand next to him. The air buzzes. You laugh too loudly and lose your balance, spill your wine like a Xanaxed bridesmaid. He grabs your wrist, you blame your heels but really you're walking a collapsing path.

You sip vodka and soda, tell him what a great husband G is. Then you say marriage isn't what you thought it would be, which hasn't occurred to you before.

'Don't get married!' you say, joking. *(Not joking.)*

'My dad's been married four times.'

You suspect he shares the gene.

'Is he an incurable romantic?'

The question shoots flares into his cheeks. You spew a girly laugh, look down at your hands, mortified. Your age spots glare back.

He tells you about someone he loved.

'Do you still love her?' you ask. You want her gone from his mind. There's a tiny tremor in your inflexion; the nosy aunt's morphing into a Roald Dahl witch. With further inquiry your back broadens, your tits plummet, hairs sprout from your nose, warts burst from your chin.

He responds in Morse Code blinks and smiles. You never learn to decipher the language.

Later he texts: No.

(Ignore it. Ignore the text.)

You reply: winking emoji, smiley face emoji xx

Month three

You're taking better care of yourself. You eat greens, exercise. The desire you feel is a mirror. Nails, highlights, kohl. You spend time smoothing facial lines and hiding veins but you can't get your face right, it's never right. People say how young you look and you tell them it's the last flush of youth and explain how dying stars burn brightest before they burn out. Rubbish, they say, but they know it's true.

You sit tall, arch your back, put your hair up, take it down. You tease like a Hogarthian whore. You're not acting your age, you're not feeling it either, and it's a wonder.

In the pub, Trouble's asleep. You tickle his ears until he's belly up. You can't stay long because it's G's birthday so it's a relief when he arrives *(it will sate you for a bit, like microdosing la petite mort.)*

You were both separated from your mothers at a young age. You say, 'It must have been especially hard for you.'

'Why?' he says.

'Boys need their mothers.' *(No filter.)*

'It was for the best.'

'But to not have a woman around.' You think of your son, how you sometimes want to run, how you never could.

'It's fine, really,' he says.

'How old were you?'

'I can't remember.'

'Jesus, that's not good.' *(Seriously, no filter.)*

You spit the truth like it's a bug your mouth. 'You seem open but you're not.' You want him to know that you get him.

He looks afraid, changes the subject. You change it back.

'How many siblings do you have?' you ask, because even though you got the hint you've taken the hint, put it in a box, buried it in the garden, and poured cement over it.

'Three sisters.'

'Same as my dad.'

He softens, you grin. *(Synchronicity, yay.)*

'Do you get on with your dad?' he asks.

'We did. He died recently, which makes me an orphan, I guess.'

He frowns like you told a bad gag. You worry your parents dying offended him or, worse, aged you. Maybe he knows a child orphan and thinks you're shamelessly trying to elicit his compassion. But he replies, 'That's tough,' and then your name, except you've never heard it said that way, imbued with special magic. You were falling and now you've fallen, you're a fallen woman and the fall has knocked the good sense out of you. You're all smiles and highs.

You ask him to explain a term you can't grasp. He does, patiently, three times.

'I'm unteachable.'

'It's in there.' He puts a long finger to your forehead. Your skin burns.

'Beeee goooood.'

'Sorry?'

'Be good, Elliott. From 'E.T.'?'

'Oh yeah, that came out before I was born.'

(Christ.)

At the restaurant, G is draining his second whisky. You're in an unforgiving mood – don't want to talk about tax returns, his backache, your backache. When you and G married you had very little and it was enough; when did it stop being enough?

G mentions an article he read, 'Apparently, this year's third most popular porn search is MILF. It's above teen in the rankings,' he says. He's citing statistical research to prove not all men letch over schoolgirls. What a sweetie.

'Why are you telling me?' You used to watch porn together; you watch it separately now.

G puts his hand on your knee and with a look of genuine concern says, 'I thought it would make you feel better.'

Month four

Food loses its flavour, your appetite wanes. Sugar and carbs no longer spark neurons in your brain, don't give the serotonin jump you get from imagining him. You have crush-induced dementia; you forget the year you married, buy the same clothes twice, order train tickets the wrong route round. At Sainsbury's it takes you 15 minutes to find the car.

The next time you meet you're agitated, your control tights chafe and your scratched scalp is sore. Your mood's a shared bird of soars and dips, you use drink like a dimmer switch.

His sister married a younger man.

'Age differences don't matter. The heart wants what it wants or else it does not care.'

'Who said that?' he asks.

(You said it.)

'Emily Dickinson.'

'What else did Emily say?' He smiles.

'We turn not older with years but newer every day.'

You're no poetry connoisseur but you've been searching for the right words and you've found it useful, like a DIY manual or bible.

'Impressive,' he says.

(You are?)

'Two of my aunts married men years younger,' you say.

'Did they have kids?'

'One couple did.'

'Did they last?'

'One couple did.'

'The one with kids?'

'The one without.'

'Do you want more kids?'

(He wants kids.)

You'd love more but you can't because you fear for your life. S's birth is a sticky red recall of buckets beneath your hips filling with thick, viscous blood, the nurse replacing one after another like you were a leak in the roof. Your pelvis is twisted like a gnarled branch, your fear for S's survival embedded in your skin like barbed wire.

'No,' you lie.

'Really?'

You picture your clear-eyed brood living in his empty chest, cosy and warm.

'I'm a terrible mother.'

(You're not, you're fierce. Coarse-tongued as a pirate but every inch is love.)

He goes to the bar without asking if you'd like a drink. Or perhaps he asks but you don't hear him because you've lost your footing on the scree and you're sliding down a mountain towards a speeding train flashing cerise underwear and stretch marks.

Too many glasses later you turn demon, feel a hot and skulking envy towards anyone who talks to him. E finds you teary-eyed in the toilet.

'You're a grown woman,' she says, not unkindly.

'You noticed?'

E nods, sympathetically.

'I've been hijacked.' In truth you're a victim of your own lust. You're Medusa, Emma Bovary, Miss Julie, but you'll never make legend.

E sees straight through this.

'Make sure it's worth it.'

You stop asking questions, you avoid eye contact. Down corridors you fall out of step with him. You give him the silent treatment, serve him with an unseen restraining order. Texts become scarce then stop.

You think of ways to hate him. He's secretive, ambiguous. You don't like his trousers.

You write a list of the things he doesn't do:
1. Tries to get to know you
2. Lets you go through a door first
3. Gets drunk with the group.

Reasons for this: head
1. He's distracted
2. He's young *(and chivalry is dead)*
3. He needs to work.

Reasons for this: heart
1. He's not interested
2. He's rude
3. His mind is on other things *(but not you)*.

It doesn't occur to you that your marriage is an impediment for him.

You spend evenings in the bath. G brings wine, asks why you're so preoccupied, but you've no time for it because you're imagining a future where you're ageless and infinitely fuckable. You hide upstairs and scour the web; Freud speaks, 'Where they love they do not desire and where they desire they cannot love.' It's this contradiction that has you stretched on a rack.

You check horoscope sites obsessively. A privacy form pops up with the words: 'Accept and move on'. You ignore the warning. On your phone, you click on tarot card after card asking for advice until the most common word in your predictive text is his name.

There are 12 years between you, 12 months in a year, 12 signs of the zodiac, 12 days of Christmas, 12 apostles, 12 hours in a day, 12 hours in a night, 12 angry men. 1 + 2 = 3 and 3 is the magic number.

More dreams; he's a psychopath, he's the devil, lips become too slippery to kiss.

You can't seem to wind yourself back up into the tight neat spool you perfected. Your scalp is a self-made scabby mess and your mind's so muddled you check for his now-non-existent texts even when he's with you.

Fortunately, you're a secret-keeper. It's because you have Scorpio rising, which you discovered while checking your horoscope obsessively. You wear the secret like a real fur stole but pass it off as faux; you bury it like magic beans but when it grows out of control you'll take an axe to it.

You're also reckless. This is the real you and she wears her cravings like ugly bruises. She doesn't belong in your organised life but she's seeping out: she toys with school-gate husbands; she walks in front of cars; she calls out the dogwalker who ignores his dog's shit and when he threatens says, 'Go on then, hit me.'

You decide fate has a bone to pick with you, find a tired-eyed therapist who says, 'Wear a hairband on your wrist and twang it when your thinking gets magical.' That night, you watch G in the kitchen – when he puts the Tupperware in the wrong cupboard you swoop in and spend 10 minutes slamming plastic.

G's response is to scold S, who's singing loudly around the house. He shushes him as if there's an injured animal in the house.

You ask, 'Do you believe in soul mates?' You think G will say you're his because he used to. You want to prove the therapist wrong.

'Load of bollocks.'

A swell of despair, then remorse.

'What the hell is wrong with you,' G says.

That night you turn to G. *(Duplicitous heart)*. At 5am you get up to check the Tupperware's still neatly stored then clean the bathroom until your cuticles bleed.

Month five

You're slimmer. This should make you happy – toddler leftovers and child-carrying gave you loadbearing hips – but you're not happy.

You write lists of his good and bad points. You print out the list of bad points, laminate it and carry it in your purse. This is what extreme dieters do – carry pictures of their bigger selves as a reminder of what not to do – so this is what you do.

You write another list – reasons to act and not act. There are 13 reasons not to act, only one to act. *(Make something happen.)*

Q&A
Q: Does he feel the same way?
A: He'd be crazy to.

Q: Is it possible to be in love with two people at the same time?
A: It's possible to think you are. *(Good answer!)*

You call E. 'It's a crush, it'll pass,' she says.
(But he's in your bones and membranes, he strobes in your brain like Cine film.)
You call your sister.
'You were like this about that singer from A-ha.'
'I was 12.'
'Are you taking your pills, sis?'
Your longing leaves a snail trail, an invisible viscid liquid on the bedding, the steering wheel, the rim of your wine glass. You're not sleeping and you're constantly questioning if the doors are locked, if the oven's off, if the alarm's on. Even when he texts – rare, polite enquiries – it's not enough. You need a text to start or end it.
(What are you waiting for? Tic tic.)
When your sister was your age she divorced, when your dad was your age he was widowed, when your mum was your age she was three years dead. They faced their fate with flashes of near-lunacy but not you, you're steady.
(But what is madness if not freedom?)

On a damp day in February you drive to Greenwich. You buy a coffee and drink it by the river. You scroll through the news on your phone, read about a captive penguin in Japan called Grape. Grape fell in love with a cardboard cutout – an anime character called Hululu – that was placed in his pen. He preened in front of it, worshipped it, he even had to be separated from it so he'd eat. Eventually, he died beside it.

Hululu was none the wiser.

You cry rickety breaths, heave grieving sighs.

You pass a new-age shop and decide to pay a clairvoyant £40. She smells of white musk and cigarettes.

'He's married,' she says.
'He's not.'
'He's a Pisces.'
'Nope.'
'Spirit says you're close to your parents, you're lucky they live nearby.'

On the way back to the car you block all psychic websites from your phone.

Month six
You don't get out of bed for three days. Your inflamed scalp stings, your wrist's raw from hairband twangs.

You watch 'South Pacific' in a duvet nest. If Nellie Forbush could wash a man right out of her hair, you can write a man out of yours. You compose a letter in the hope it will make you feel better. It doesn't.

You realise the places you planned to visit with G, frozen places – Alaska, Iceland – you want to escape to with him. But he'd see you hyperventilating on a plane and be appalled. And when you fucked he'd see your stretch marks and be appalled. G loves you regardless.

You tell G you're bereft because you'll never feel passion again. Then you forget you said it. *(Can't take that back.)* You're a better fantasist than a wife.

You want him but since when has wanting been enough?

G sits on the bed and insists you go back on your pills.

'Why?' You accuse G of being like a controlling Victorian husband, tell him he's the type who'd commit his wife to an asylum for having PMT.

G looks hurt but undeterred.

'You remind me of a glass,' he says, eventually.

'What?' G has called you many things but never a glass.

'A glass that wants to shatter.'

'And what good would that be?'

'Then you'd scatter, live all the lives you need.'

You wonder if G has also turned to poetry.

G squeezes your hand, goes downstairs and returns with a bowl of tomato soup. S comes in, lies down beside you and reads you a story about a monkey who loses her baby.

On the third day you realise that each interaction with him felt like the last. It was too regular a replay of grief. It's where you put your grief.

You couldn't find a way to know him better. Perhaps this was his intention. Perhaps it was yours.

You thought you needed a new beginning to offset the endings but what's needed is another ending. The good news is it's like S's Choose Your Own Adventure books – you decide. The bad news is you're frozen, petrified. Like Alaska and Iceland.

Love is a punch to the throat. Love is a battlefield. Love is a losing game. Your love doesn't have limits but you do. You see the doctor; she writes a repeat prescription. You walk to the pharmacy – it's snowing, spring isn't ready to spring yet – and when your fingers go numb you consider removing your clothes so your whole body is anaesthetised.

At home you turn the familiar box over in your hands. Soon the fixations will fade.

Love is a tic. Love is madness. Love is an illness so treat it like one.

'You'll be back to your old self before you know it,' G says.

(Your old self?)

'Sure,' you say.

SHORT STORY SECOND PRIZE

CARA GEORGE

Fight, Flight, Freeze, Comply, Film (FFFCF)

The birds were where they always were. In the trees or nests or flittering around in the fallen leaves or stabbing the earth for worms. The rest were in the air, between places.

Then all the birds flew straight up. Every bird that could fly, flew. They went higher than the scientists thought they could. To ice-making altitudes and then beyond. Shooting skywards in one immediate motion. They left.

There was a global call to take shelter as it was predicted solid carcasses would rain down, killing instantly upon impact. People locked out hated spouses and unwanted pets in the hope that they would be crushed by a frozen blackbird. Nothing fell back to Earth.

The scientists could not explain where the birds went. Atomised, some said. Realm shifted, said others.

People filmed The Great Flight. People everywhere because there was not a place on Earth free from the sudden flight of the birds. And apparently there was nowhere on Earth free from cameras.

Footage even came out of a patch of Amazon rainforest that still stood. Scarlet macaws, plum-throated cotingas, speckled owls, yellow-crowned caracaras, vultures and cobalt kingfishers lifted themselves from the canopies forever. The treetops quivered and bounced back, lightened of their load.

The rainforest videos amazed anthropologists more than ornithologists but no one was more surprised than the telecommunications people.

In places that it was daytime and cloudless, the full shape of the sky, usually so empty, could be seen. Replete with birds, the sky was noted by some to look quite small. The revelation about the size of the sky could only be witnessed for the few minutes before the sun was blotted out. Day became feather-clogged. In the places that it was night time, the stars and moon were ghosted away.

Hundreds of planes crashed as unceasing waves of birds missiled into their engines. Feathered corpses, avian and human, landed on houses and roads and killed the many who came out to watch. A video of a dismembered, charred leg that landed and bounced on a trampoline was uploaded online. The bouncing leg clip had been looped to *Jump Around* by House of Pain. The footage was removed several times before all video channels were temporarily disabled. If people couldn't be tasteful and sensitive, the government said, then liberty for all must be paused.

Captive birds hurled themselves into the rafters of the barns and the bars of the cages they were kept in with deathly determination. Squads of Avian Clean Up Teams (ACUT) were assembled. Forensic scientists, the army and birdwatchers were called upon to assist.

The air pressure changed, they told us later. Millions of wings pushing down like that. People said they felt instantly depressed. Even the happiest of people reported feeling heavily sad. There were videos of spontaneous, collective suicide, so rapid it looked joyous.

The videos were taken down from one online platform only to emerge on another, haunting the internet with liquid ease. There were rumours of 'avian suicide' being contagious. People started to prepare. Do Not Resuscitate forms were given out at pharmacies. At first, the government boosted funding for the Samaritans and similar charities. Later the funding was channelled into building emergency morgues.

International efforts were made. Large investments were funnelled into incubation labs. All eggs were seized, wild or otherwise. Nothing hatched.

Scientists tried to create birds, harvesting DNA from the swathes of feathers that rained down during The Great Flight. Great Flight Replication Centres were set up to simulate the event and determine the cause. The hope was a reversal could be triggered. The centres were quietly dismantled after a few years.

Google reported a surge in searches for collective nouns to describe gatherings of different bird species. Top searches included hummingbirds (a bouquet, charm, hover, glittering, shimmer, tune) and woodpeckers (a descent, drumming, fall, gatling). The most online searches were made for birds that prefer solitude.

CCTV from zoos went viral. A flamboyance of flamingos in China flew repeatedly into the expanse of netting that enclosed them. Eventually the flamingos dislodged the mesh but became ensnared. They managed to get airborne. A tangle of flapping pink panic ascended. A peacock in London Zoo who couldn't escape plucked all its feathers out. People videoed pet budgies slamming into their cage rooves. Many people filmed all the way to the end, zooming in to capture the lifeless feathery mess of blood. Fight, flight, freeze, comply. Disaster psychologists added 'film' to the list after studying hours of footage that surfaced online.

The flightless birds all stopped singing. Then stopped eating. Like fasting mystics, they vanished too but more slowly. The government developed Benevolent Avian Assisted Suicide Scheme (BAASS) because the public were becoming distressed at the sight of rotting, skeletal sparrows and blue tits littering their gardens. Defunct chicken farms were repurposed into industrial avian incinerators. Some of the birdwatchers refused to help with the round up but most agreed it was the kindest plan of action.

All the eggs in the world sold out within 27 hours of The Great Flight. There was a national Memorial Omelette Day. People cooked their last eggs in the shapes of crosses and wore black at breakfast.

NASA said there was no evidence that the birds made it as far as the Earth's atmosphere. On the anniversary of The Great Flight, astronauts recorded a flash of colour around Earth. The colour changed every year but no method to capture the event succeeded. The scientists called it spectrum resistance. The faithful called it God's promise. The sceptics didn't believe the phenomenon happened at all.

In the weeks immediately afterwards, children and probably some adults, drew bird wings on windows. People started to wear beak masks. There was a touch of the plague about everything.

People changed their ringtones to birdsong. Shopping centres and supermarkets swapped music for the dawn chorus. The government commissioned civil engineers to create speakers that could be hidden in parks and greenspaces. Birdsong flooded the cities. People in rural locations complained that they had to travel to urban places or shops to hear the birds sing again. A radio station that exclusively played birdsong was introduced to the air waves.

At the beginning, people remembered how to hunt. Forests and hedgerows teemed with humans clambering into trees, shaking branches to release any nests and abandoned eggs. No one managed to rear a new bird. Children buried the last of the unhatched in eggbox coffins.

The bio-engineers tried to artificially inseminate platypuses hoping their eggs could be hijacked and repurposed to birth birds. The platypuses crushed any eggs that emerged. The scientists created contraptions to prevent the mammals destroying their eggs. The eggs were empty anyway.

People hacked up paving stones splattered in bird excrement and sold them in chunks for huge sums, much like the Berlin wall was siphoned off.

'Plumage' started to be used in conversation to mean a rare or unlikely event. *Fat plumage he'll be faithful.*

Fight, Flight, Freeze, Comply, Film (FFFCF)

Tinned Confit de Canard was sold for its weight in gold.

A craze for 'nest' hairstyles took off. Plaits woven into circular coils. Extensions for those who wanted to partake but had been disthatched of their own crop. Shaven depressions into full heads of hair. Hairbands scattered with tiny plastic birds. For a few years it felt like a continual Easter bonnet competition.

People bought T-shirts with phrases on like AVIAN FLEW, ON A WING & PRAYER, and FEATHERLITE.

Musicians staged a global farewell concert. A little late some said. Orchestras in every time zone played a symphony at daybreak and dusk. The choruses of their native birdsong for the start and end of the day. Nightingales and cockerels.

For a while, chocolate manufacturers stopped making bars and only produced confectionary in the shape of eggs and feathers. Kinder Egg sales rocketed and then plummeted.

The Pope prayed in private. Then he prayed harder in public, on his weak knees, for forty days. And then again for forty nights. Finally, he lay prostrate on the ground and begged Saint Francis to intercede and talk the birds back. *Solo una colomba.* Not even a pigeon returned.

David Attenborough said I told you so.

Chris Packham tweeted to say this was just the beginning.

The last of the goose-down duvets and pillows were bought in one multi-billion-dollar transaction by an anonymous private buyer. The middle-poor cleared mortgages by selling their feather-filled bed linen to the middle-rich. The price of synthetic bedding tripled overnight as it was no longer the cheaper option. Some nests were feathered, some beds became colder.

People gave their children new names. The most popular name for a boy was Eagle and for a girl, Dove. Dodo, Ostrich and Albatross were also common.

Tattoos of feathers started to emerge on backs and necks. Little trendy angel wings tucked behind ears. A flutter of quills on smooth juvenile wrists.

There was an RSPB RIP event.

The MP in charge of social control systems and promotional messages of hope (and warning) was publicly shamed after a drone-camera filmed her PA stock piling free-range eggs during the aftermath.

A homing pigeon champion said he tried to warn everyone. They were flitty, he said, the day before they all flew away. Wouldn't leave the coop. Like they were afraid or preparing.

Cats went mad for a while, with nothing to hunt they started to torment each other. Cat on cat crime went up. Gradually they stopped wanting to breed. Chris Packham said I told you so. David Attenborough retired.

Legislation was changed to give the police more power. Avian Related Hate Speech (ARHS) was a crime that carried an instant hefty fine. All profits, the government promised, went into funding Bird Replacement Research Programmes.

There were riots. The police patrolled the streets to split up the meat-eaters from the climateers. Chicken shops were double-targets. Raided for the last of the chicken nuggets and torched for being the cause. WE TOLD YOU THEY HAD FEELINGS AND WINGS was sprayed across KFC shops in a nationally synced vegan graffiti protest.

The government said we had to Keep Calm And Carry On. The Queen said we've done it before, we can do it again.

The campaign was quickly changed to Keep Calm And Move On. 'Carry On' was thought to be too similar to 'carrion' and so moving on was firmly encouraged. Carrying on as normal was no longer spoken of. Panic had to be avoided. People complained about the buses emblazoned with the old motto triggering anxiety attacks.

Someone found an unreleased Prince song called *The Day The Birds Left*. An international vigil was held as the song played for the first time on the radio. Fans waved feathers aloft instead of candles and painted PRINCE WAS A PROPHET across their glittered cheeks.

There were reports of birds flying over the polar icecaps but they were found to be fake and the teenage hackers involved were charged with the crime of Inciting Avian Related False Hope (IARFH) and then enlisted to help at the Bird Replacement Research Programmes.

People started to worry that all winged creatures would leave. They tried to build netting systems around areas of outstanding natural beauty. To keep the bees and butterflies safe, they said. To keep them trapped, others said. Move on, move on.

'Ghosting' was replaced by 'birding'. The lover who vanishes.

SHORT STORY THIRD PRIZE

DAFYDD MILLS DANIEL

What the Deal is

Sheriff Tom said he'd been driving by some carwash owned by a Mexican just out on this lot where they parked cars stacked up like you might have seen in these open crates
and he'd been driving past this place just as a matter of course at first but now he's been getting to doing it for watching
says he's seen all these cars just getting themselves clean even though they was as sparkling as they was when they was born
some queuing to go through the machine with all them red and blue rolls coming right across your car and others just waiting to get out and spray the car themselves with a pressure hose and make sure you get at the tyres and all that
well at first Sheriff Tom says he thinks nothing of it but then when he keeps seeing all these people cleaning their cars that don't need cleaning he just thinks what the hell and the next day figures if he sees all these cars still he'll go and ask what's what
so the next day he pulls up not in uniform and goes across to see what all this is all about.

Says the Mexican was called Raul Mejia though he finds this out later and that as he walks out across this lot this Mexican says to him clean your car like he was just talking to some good old boy and Sheriff Tom says well goddamn seems like half North Carolina come down here for the cleaning and the Mexican says yessir and Sheriff Tom says well what you think gets them to do that then and the Mexican says I don't know and Sheriff Tom says is that right
well eventually the Mexican says something about their loyalty bonus says well everyone here wants to get that bonus it's the American way
and I don't know if he did ever say that last bit but you can see just what he was trying to do and how he was trying to sound
Sheriff Tom says he's seen this here thing about this loyalty bonus underneath the sign of all the different prices of the cleaning so what is this bonus

the Mexican tells him you clean your car ten times you get our bonus
Sheriff Tom says okay but what is this bonus
says the Mexican seemed to take it okay
says I'll show you
Sheriff Tom thinking maybe he's a bit too keen to show him
doesn't say it's just the usual kinda thing or even get angry and go hey what is this you get your car cleaned you find out
but then maybe that's not even the way a Mexican deals with a could be paying customer
and for Sheriff Tom even that sort of answer could have meant something funny in its own way
so this Mexican takes him over to his office and says you get one free wash and one of these and shows the Sheriff this lighter with an eagle on it and a white china mug with just some pattern across it
and the Sheriff says alright and good luck to you son and maybe I'll see you for a clean sometime or whatever it is he would have said just walking away.

Anyway as you're thinking Sheriff Tom was
was thinking these people standing all these cars deep with all their sparkling goodness to go after some lighter and a china mug
it didn't set right with him
didn't seem like nothing consistent with anything at all
so Sheriff Tom thinks it's time to come for a proper look round
thinking it must be drugs and whatever else and maybe not just because the guy was Mexican but because what else is all these people doing washing them cars up over and over
so Sheriff Tom said they just come back along towards evening he and his Deputy Willard and that the place is all closed up but Raul's in there in his office and Sheriff Tom wasn't sure if he really recognised him or not so he says to him how's business
and this Mexican says we just gone shut up couple hours ago
and Sheriff Tom says well I'm just getting to wondering about all your cars
and the Mexican says it's our loyalty bonus I done told you
and so Sheriff Tom knows that the Mexican knows him and so he smiles and says yessir you did but I'm just thinking how many lighters and mugs does a man need anyway
so they set about having a good look round.

What the Deal is

They thought most of all said Sheriff Tom about them cars stacked up there but they thought not to go messing around with them at first
the Mexican said they weren't his anyway
that that was a separate business run and rented by someone else on the lot
and they were a bit worried about getting anywhere then without coming back again because they weren't sure if what the Mexican said was true and they were thinking maybe one of them cars stacked up there was just plumb full of cocaine
but that didn't worry them for long because Willard saw this storehouse at the back of the lot behind the Mexican's office and they said it was a pretty big looking storehouse for what it was as there was only this little office the Mexican sat in and then the pressure hoses and the big drive through cleaning machine and so they thought they may as well take a look in there
and so Sheriff Tom is talking to his Deputy
saying yup that looks like a pretty big storehouse to me
and the Mexican says it's where they keep the spare rolls
and it was clear to them that the Mexican had no idea what he was talking about
though none of them knew for sure how much liquids and rolls and whatever else you might need to run that machine and all them hoses out there
so the Mexican just led them over to the storehouse and opened the lock on the front and walked them in leading the way.

Sheriff said there was nothing unusual in that for him and he's right most often about that
you don't know what it is but people will lead you over to their own evil without a word
like they expect that it's gone away or that you might not even notice it for what it is when you get there
like maybe they hadn't noticed it for what it was themselves yet and so didn't think one odd thought about it
yes that's what the Sheriff said even about this Mexican
said that he'd known people doing things that guess the people coming asking are the law so that they done clean their way out so when they stay they haven't guessed it yet
or it's just that you get to doing something long enough no matter what it is that it just don't seem like it's gonna end

it seems like it's complete and real and everlasting and as solid as the fist in your hand and to doubt it being allowed to go on is like doubting yourself and the colour of dirt
and that that Mexican most likely just wasn't thinking about getting caught even if he'd known Sheriff Tom for what he was when he'd been up on him earlier that day
either that or the Sheriff had come back and got him just as he was fixing to leave
but most likely that Mexican didn't think one way questioning about it
except maybe that there was luck to ride and it wasn't his choice when to stop riding
that it wasn't up to him when the luck ran out.

So anyway the Sheriff and his Deputy walked right on into the storehouse and from what they said at first at least it wasn't as bad as you might have thought in that there's worse places for that kind of thing and the people there look worse sometimes but when you thought about it and stood in it longer it could seem just as bad
because although there never came a time for asking about certain things because other things is more important once the law gets moving
the things you thought about later strike you just as bad and make the whole thing worse than it could ever have looked at first and breed all kinds of cruel imaginings
like the Sheriff said there was no place for a toilet they could see or a shower so he never found out what they did about that and why it didn't smell so bad as you might have thought knowing that and so you have to say that some things are just far worse than you ever can tell and there's no glimmering relief in a first look to be held on to that might tell you it could be worse
that all you have to know is that ever thing is pushing itself into this great big lump of hatred and you can't look at it the same when you find it in its pieces but it all belongs in the same shape.

So they walked into that place behind this Mexican and what they had in front of them was on one side a wall of metal shelving with rolled up hosing and wire on it and boxes of cleaner and clear tubing and in one corner something like the Sheriff said were blue plastic barrels standing on the floor like the things you might find filled with oil and a few gas

What the Deal is

canisters and that kind of thing and three women just set there against the wall in front of them who looked up at them as they came in

and Sheriff Tom said as they looked back at them after they secured the Mexican one of them girls just stood up and walked out through a little doorway without a door that was in the wall they were set against and just waited in there for a short time and then came back on in and set back down

Sheriff Tom guessing she wasn't sure what they was there for if they hadn't followed her in

maybe got undressed and dressed again and just thought what the hell or as was most likely as it was how she looked hadn't thought anything at all.

That girl was herself Mexican and Sheriff Tom said she looked young but only maybe because all three looked any age you could have picked

and when that Mexican girl come back in and she set back down the girl in the middle of the three just starts screaming all this wild stuff and noise standing up and setting back down and finally deciding on standing up and just screaming with these mystic words with God knows what dark light for all the spirits she was bent on creating and asking

this girl was Asian and Sheriff Tom said he thought Chinese at first but you could take your pick

and he said that she stood up screaming alongside this white girl who had stood up first

and that this white girl was standing already even before the Mexican girl stood up slowly and walked back in and out from that other room

and that this white girl had stood up as soon as they'd come in because you couldn't come in and see these women in front of you and think nothing about it so that Raul was turned and pressed right up against the wall at gun point and cuffed as soon as they were in

and that it was right away then that this white girl had moved and stood there with nothing on naked and just awful in the awful nothing light of that place

and she just stood to the left of the Asian girl screaming and that Mexican girl

all three just there with these blankets on the floor in front of them and empty and half-full bad looking gallon jugs of water and foil boxes with plastic forks in them

and this white girl just stood leaning on her left shoulder against the wall with her head tilted sideways against the wall over her left shoulder

and Sheriff Tom said it seemed like she was sometimes looking up at him and Willard and at other times like she was looking off at some low point down somewhere in the corner of the room
and that it seemed like she would look up a little at them and then back down along her angle but that wherever she was looking it always looked like she was just staring down anyway or just not even staring at all
like her eyes were just open and that all that went in went in just to no where if it even went in at all.

So Sheriff Tom just looks at all this and says to them out loud what the hell is all this
saying it again to the Mexican first of all when no one else says nothing and then to them girls
Sheriff Tom said that when he asked them what the hell is all this Raul the Mexican said I don't know and Sheriff Tom said later it was like the funniest thing he ever heard anyone say and that as no one was saying nothing he told them they was all under arrest and sent Willard out with the Mexican to set him in the squad car and tells him to call this in
but says that fore he'd done that he'd gone over to the Chinese girl screaming while Willard was still there holding the Mexican against the wall
said he'd gone across to her and felt like nothing in the wake of her forces and her words and said to her ma'am ma'am it's okay or something that was nothing like that and she just went right on screaming up from hell
so he just put out his hand and thought that maybe at the time he'd pushed her down somehow but knew that he'd only just barely touched her but she went straight down anyway and set there silent not moving nothing at all
and the Sheriff said he looked down at her there set next to the Mexican girl and looked back up and couldn't but look right into that white girl leaning there and just wasn't sure whether she was looking at him or even whether he was looking at her
that as he looked at her eyes he wasn't sure there was any sight left in the world at all
so he turned slightly and leaned down in front of her and picked up the blanket nearest to her because if that's where she'd come up from if anything there belonged to anyone that was what belonged to her
and after that Chinese girl he didn't want to get too much in the way of what they were
so he just held out the blanket to her

What the Deal is

and the Sheriff said that she looked at him in her nothing way so he reached out the blanket to her and hung it over her shoulder and still nothing in her or about her seemed to move so the blanket slid right off her and she stood there again naked in her finality and he bent down to pick it up and picked it up a little and looked up a little at her and just dropped that blanket right back down.

Turned out later the white girl was somewhere from eastern Europe and the Chinese girl was Vietnamese and what was happening was when you got your ten washes through the machine or fifteen on them hoses you could claim your bonus and your bonus was to come out in to that storeroom and lie with one of them girls while the Mexican cleaned your car with the pressure hose
that them girls took it in turns going out with each guy round through into that little room without a door because it was a space no bigger than the flat double mattress shoved in on the floor
and them girls took it in turns with that same bit of mattress sleeping in there of a night if they'd had enough of the floor and blankets in the main part and if it got too cold they'd all go in there together and share that mattress but they tended to stay sleeping together out of that room.

Sheriff Tom said all this is what the different lawyers who'd been with the translators told him but he wouldn't be sure they'd slept ever and he'd asked them what it was they did all the time and said he was told they couldn't be sure how long they'd been there but it looked like they could communicate okay somehow
that the European and the Vietnamese could speak a bit of French and they could all speak a bit of English and they all seemed to have just talked at each other and sung some things but that it seemed to ADA Wilson who brought in the FBI that they'd mostly just set there and taken it and been together somehow
and he'd said that about them being together because when they'd put them all together in the processing cell at the county lockup to make deciding on translators easier as they come through to speak to them all at once they'd all three set there along the wall and were holding hands
and he'd said that about singing because you could see them moving their lips together sometimes muttering some thing like a tune shared between them

though he couldn't really say for sure that they weren't just talking to themselves
and he didn't know what was going to happen to them all now but none of them had any permits or nothing so they'd most likely be going back to someplace sometime and that goddamn nothing was right and nothing was good and he couldn't even imagine it all at all and what else can you do about it and what else is anyone else gonna do about it and what in Christ's name could you do about it all anyway
Sheriff Tom said Wilson seemed quite animated about it and he felt bad about it for him and many other things beside and just kept saying to him yessir and I just don't know at all
and it's true that you just don't know what that's all about
like how even that Mexican had got them girls together
where he'd found them or been given them from
whether he'd built them up slow so that one had been there the longest and was senior in that place
and I am sorry to put it like it's nothing like that and it's just curious somehow because of course it's more than that besides but it is that too itself somehow
like Sheriff Tom said they'd gotten some video footage from the security cameras of that place and you could see these fellers claiming their reward getting out their cars and handing them over to the Mexican who led them out to the storehouse and then he'd come back and clean their cars and he said it was funny and no one ever told him different but so far as he knew from what he'd seen on them videos no man ever came on out refusing from that place
and maybe that was already clear from what he'd said as no one had ever called it in
but not calling it in didn't necessarily mean nothing about the judgement of an individual
and it's true that there are things beyond all holiness and fear that people see and don't call in because they just don't believe what's right in front of them
they're stunned not even morally just stunned and nothing in them at all could make them even consider or understand what it would mean to act on something that was beyond all possibility of understanding
but not once did someone come running on out of that place
course people was in there for differing times
but what we think of ourselves doing if some Mexican says I've got this loyalty bonus for you you just follow me out to this here storehouse out back

What the Deal is

I'd say he was out of his goddamn mind
that I wasn't following him no place at all
that he was crazier than hell
and you know maybe there were ones like that who said no thank you sir
and got the mug or the lighter but you would have thought that someone
might be in between you know and just say alright curious like
like maybe this is some here big king bonus being kept out in a storehouse
some place
but you'd walk in behind that Mexican into that place and say no thank
you sir and run like a demon on fire
and of course maybe there was some that were scared thinking if I don't
stay in this place that Mexican out there is going to get me and I've just got
to set here for five ten minutes and look like I've done when I come on out
and just never think about this here little devil's cove hole ever again
and we don't know how many done that
how many just set there like that not knowing what to do and just left and
got the blazes out of there
but you know what I think more than I like is that someone like that may
have set in there thinking that and then seen that Mexican girl rise up and
go on out into that room and through curiosity or instinct or fear or relief
or wonder just get up and follow that girl for no one single thought or idea
they could explain to themselves later but just follow that girl and see her
lay down and thought nothing or God knows what as they got down with
her there themselves.

In the end they rounded up a lot of them guys tracing number plates
who knows if it come as a surprise to them and whether it was or it wasn't
you can't understand it either way
I heard it told that one of them they picked up said he'd never got to sleep
with one of them girls
made a bit of a fuss about it too
like having a grievance about it made it less of something somehow
said he'd gone in and said he wanted the Mexican girl as he'd already
been with the Vietnamese and the white girl twice and now the
Vietnamese was going into that room again
said he said all kinds of things but neither the European nor the Mexican
moved and the Vietnamese had already gone through to lie down
said he just accepted it but saw no reason why it should've been like that
like he felt they were choosing when he wasn't able but they acted like
they weren't choosing neither

as though some power had made it the way it was and that power was above them as much as him and they couldn't control it when the way it was was up to them
by all accounts sounded like it did that feller some good to get that frustration off his chest
don't know what frustrations it caused when no one else saw his side of things
whether he kept hold tight to his own injustice and just saw his arrest as an extension of it
people like that it's beyond all comprehension what time they're given to think twice that they don't take and what they fill up that time with rather than thinking about who they are and what they done
take all those fellers set out there in their cars just waiting
Sheriff Tom said on the videos you could see them just set there in their cars waiting for their turn with the pressure hose or else them girls
just setting there waiting with their radios on
maybe having a smoke as well
just setting there waiting for that Mexican to come on over and get them
take that Mexican as well
Tom said that Mexican would turn off the hose when he seen them coming out of the storehouse having just kindly danced that hose over their car that was already clean from all them other washes anyway
but what was he doing that for at all while he waited for them
like he had to go through the motions of the deal and give them that one free clean otherwise all wasn't right in the world and with business
that Mexican's head as nothing and as empty and as dead as those girl's eyes
Tom even said on the video you could see some of these same cars coming back four five times a day to get their loyalty bonus and get to them girls that that Mexican had his whole business built up on his returning customers and his loyalty scheme and that sometimes you could even see him giving a little wave to the car driving off wet from the hose he just sprayed over it but you couldn't tell if any of his customers ever did wave back
I'd like to think they didn't do that and I'm not saying that if they didn't there was shame and that it changes anything even if there was
like if they couldn't wave because they wouldn't let themselves think about what they'd done and tried to ignore it somehow and then weren't surprised when they was picked up
but what it comes to is you have to accept that some of them and maybe all of them did wave back and that if they didn't they didn't just because they didn't care to not from anything else besides

What the Deal is

that some of them most likely smiled about it too even if it was just to themselves and that they smiled about it ordinarily like thinking about a beer over lunch
that they most likely never thought about it in any other way than just in the manner of things
and you know there was one last thing
or if you want to put it like that maybe it was the first and maybe all these things are first and last and make all that's beginning and of the end but it turned out that that Mexican taking his customers with the loyalty bonus back and round never once took no black guy back there
said that following the footage anyway there was never any sign of it and from what they could tell them other boys would just be given a lighter or a mug and be sent on their way
Sheriff Tom said he never asked Wilson about that
said he just let him tell it to him and got the impression that Wilson just let the Mexican tell it to him also
that Wilson didn't really ask the Mexican nothing about it either so that both Wilson and the Sheriff just accepted what was trivial like it was final and spoke to some end or truth in this abomination
like somehow you couldn't question that as much as anything else
like somehow there was at least something familiar in that way of hating when it made just as little sense to the emptiness of it all as anything else besides.

ERIKA BANERJI

She Came to Stay

In September 1974, a year after we moved from Kolkata to England, Ruby Miller came to stay as our lodger in the attic room of the house we rented on Maple Drive. My mother hated the idea of a stranger in our home but my father insisted.

'There is no other way to earn some extra money,' he said and his word was as always, final.

Our new home was a red-brick Victorian, set in a hollow against the South Downs. The steps leading from the road to the flaking white front door were steep and narrow. Adults with large feet had trouble walking up that flight of steps, but my parents never had that problem. We are a small-footed family.

I was nine years old when we moved to England and all I'd known until that year was the ancestral house in Bhawanipur where we lived with my father's extended family. Mothers and fathers, Aunts and Uncles, and a bushel of cousins all lived under one roof in a neighbourhood teeming with people and passing traffic. However late or early it was, there was always a background of voices or music or the incessant beeping of horns.

Maple Drive couldn't have been more different; its row of narrow brick houses and closed-curtained windows, and silent, stone-faced neighbours, a place that, in every sense, was indifferent to our presence.

Our next-door-neighbours, Mr. and Mrs. Mayo, a middle-aged retired couple spent a lot of time working on their knees in the garden and didn't look up when they saw us. The young couple a few doors down didn't wave or chat when they got in and out of their car and saw my mother bringing home heavy bags of shopping, and not one of our neighbours paid us a visit.

When I woke in the morning, dressed and got ready for school, the silence in the house was eerie. No grandmother calling me down for breakfast, no Hindi songs playing on the radio or voices rising from the maids in the kitchen, no chatter between my aunts and mother, and most of all, no children playing quick rounds of French cricket in the dusty street outside.

She Came to Stay

One evening, a week before Ruby arrived, I was setting out the plates and cutlery on the small kitchen table where we ate all our meals. Baba came home from work and was ready for his dinner after a long shift at the insurance office in Crawley. He tapped his fingers on the side of his plate and stared at Mamoni's back as she stirred a pot of yellow *daal*. The air smelt of popped cumin seeds and burnt ghee.

'Baba, will our lodger be eating with us?'

'Yes, Tulsi she will eat with us.' He rolled up his shirtsleeves in anticipation of the food. 'She will live with us as part of the family.'

Mamoni served the ridged bitter gourd. She wore a long grey cardigan over her sari; the sleeves turned up at the cuffs, stained with yellow turmeric. Her red and white bangles clattered against the side of the pot as she lifted the spoon. There were dark circles under her eyes.

'I still don't see why we need to have a lodger in the house?' Mamoni said, raising her chin towards the kitchen door as if someone was about to walk in that minute.

Baba ignored her and ate, always first to be served, first to eat, never waiting for anybody else to finish, and he always left his plate at the table for Mamoni to clear away. She glanced in his direction and I could tell from the tightness of her mouth that she was angry.

'But will she be able to eat something like this?' I asked as Mamoni put a spoonful of the gourd on my plate. I hated the bitterness of the vegetable, but Baba made loud smacking sounds with his lips as he ate. Mamoni took a bus every Monday to the Indian grocery store in Tooting to buy it. It took her two hours to get there and back.

'She will, the British are no strangers to India. Think of all those years they ruled us,' he said.

'Okay,' I said, 'but...'

'Listen carefully, Tulsi, we renamed so many of our dishes to suit them like kedgeree, and mulligatawny. It can't be that unfamiliar.' He mixed the rice and daal with his fingers, shaping little mounds onto the side of his plate.

I thought he was wrong but didn't dare argue. I wished Mamoni would make something like mashed potatoes and peas or fish-fingers for a change. This was what my friend Sarah's mother always served for tea whenever she invited me over.

I asked no one back to our house.

It wasn't just the food that I was worried about. I was sure the way my parents shouted at each other would embarrass our guest. This happened mostly at mealtimes.

Mamoni hadn't given up asking Baba about going back to Kolkata. She blamed him for how much our circumstances had changed since we'd left.

They always ended up arguing. Sometimes, after an argument, I found her sitting alone on her bed, wiping her tears as she stared out at the windowless, grey building of the Kitty-Kat pet food factory across the road.

The night before Ruby came, Baba gave Mamoni strict instructions at the top of his voice, like a schoolmaster scolding a child. He thought I was asleep and had no idea that, from my room next door, I could hear every word.

'If you're nervous about your English,' he said, 'you must ask Tulsi to translate for you.'

I felt important when I heard this but later, when I was nearly asleep, and after Baba finished telling Mamoni what to do and say to Ruby, I felt ashamed. They were shouting at each other and something fell with a loud thump, then silence. I didn't dare go out to the hall. Baba had forbidden me to knock on their door after my bedtime, and so I stayed still and quiet in the darkness and hoped Mamoni was okay. Later, I heard her feet on the floorboards as she went downstairs to the living room, as she did most nights.

Ruby was to arrive the following afternoon. It was a Wednesday, the last week of September. The pavements on Maple Drive were scattered with the first fall of yellow leaves.

I knew hardly anything about Ruby then, only that she was almost thirty and had a job that would pay the rent. In time, the idea of her moving in thrilled me. Maybe we'd become friends, me and Ruby.

Baba gave Mamoni some extra housekeeping money that week and I could see that he was pleased about the added income that was soon to come in. According to Baba, having a lodger in this day and age was a perfectly respectable practice, especially with all the inconvenience caused by miners' strikes and tiresome picketing at factories and the constant power cuts that year.

As usual, it was Mamoni who picked me up after school that Wednesday afternoon. It was almost exactly a year since we had arrived in England and the sun was low over the hills of the South Downs. As we headed home, up the Godstone Road, past Lloyd's newsagent where Mamoni bought her milk, and the fish and chip shop with the pickled eggs in the window with the grey statue of a charity sheepdog next to the door, I sensed there was something different about Mamoni. She walked faster than usual, her sari swishing against her ankles. I caught the occasional flash of the blue leggings she'd borrowed from Baba and wore

She Came to Stay

underneath. I noticed she had, for a change, applied a bit of make-up; lipstick and black liner, her dark eyes bold and wide.

'Are you looking forward to meeting our new lodger?' I said.

'Maybe,' she said, 'it might be nice to have some company in the house after all.'

I held her hand to cross the road at the edge of the Downs and she kept on smiling into nothing, her lips moving silently, and I wondered if, like me, she was practicing what to say to Ruby.

Our house looked prouder too, as if it was waiting for our guest. In the small front garden, the sunflower I had planted early that summer drooped its head, pregnant with seeds. A stray cash and carry bag fluttered against the withered hydrangea bush. Next door, Mr and Mrs Mayo had piled up bags of cut grass against their wall and an orange lawnmower stood on the slope of their perfectly clipped front lawn.

Inside, Mamoni had cooked an array of extravagant dishes, each one presented in her best crockery, the blue and gold embossed ones my grandmother had so carefully wrapped for her when we were leaving. Somehow, in the kitchen here, with the red floors and formica table, they didn't look as grand as they did in the house in Bhawanipur. It made me sad, and I wished that Mamoni hadn't put them out.

Mamoni had opened all the doors and windows and filled the rooms with incense sticks which she stuck into halved potatoes, now oxidised and blue at the edges. The smell of sandalwood and sweet jasmine wafted in every room.

Ruby was due at five o'clock. At four, I went up to my room and changed into my best clothes I kept for special days, a red checked skirt and a white nylon blouse with a lace collar. I came down to wait with Mamoni in the kitchen.

We played cards at the kitchen table for a few minutes, but she couldn't sit still long enough to finish a game and went out to bring in the washing.

It was nearly five-thirty, and I pretended to work on my English essay but I was just as restless as Mamoni and every few minutes I went into the front room and looked through the curtains to check for taxis and buses. All I saw was a delivery truck reverse into the factory across the road, and Mr. Mayo clipping at his perfect hedge. There was no sign of Ruby.

Ruby was late and it was nearly dark so I switched on our black and white telly and stretched out on the carpet to watch Blue Peter.

It was six o'clock when the doorbell rang. Mamoni checked her hair in the mirror. 'She's here,' she said, 'Turn off the television.'

'Will I let her in?'

'Yes, you must.'
I opened the door and Ruby was checking the soles of her shoes.
'Are you Ruby?' I said.
She looked up at me, surprised but not embarrassed.
'Oh,' she said. 'That was quick, you must have been waiting for me.'
Her hair was frizzy and golden and she was tall, really tall, at least six feet. She wore flared jeans and a low-cut striped top under a red coat. I couldn't help thinking that she looked like the busker we often saw standing at the corner of East Croydon station.
'Please come in,' I said. 'Let me help with your bags.'
'Aren't you sweet,' she said.
Mamoni pulled her sari tight round her shoulders and stood beside me. 'Welcome to your new home,' she said. Her words sounded rehearsed.
It was much darker now, colder too, and the air smelt of rain. I turned on the hallway lights.
'Thank you Mrs. Basu,' said Ruby. 'Here I am with all my stuff, as promised.'

Ruby walked quick and straight into the narrow hallway and waved her large hands about when she spoke. We put her luggage on the red and gold *kantha* rug we'd brought all the way from Kolkata. There wasn't much luggage: one grey suitcase covered in stickers, a basket and a black musical instrument case but I remember how the house suddenly seemed even smaller, somehow shrunken.
Mamoni helped with the bags and cases. Ruby didn't offer to help.
'It smells nice in here,' said Ruby as she stepped into the lounge. 'Are you a great cook, Mrs. Basu? I really hope you are. I can't wait to try some exotic Indian food.'
Mamoni giggled.
'No, no, I cook for family. My husband enjoying his home food.'
Ruby looked down at me.
'So, are you going to introduce yourself young lady?' she said, and I blushed.
'Hey, I've got a feeling you and I are going to be great friends.' She rummaged in her coat pocket and brought out a foil-wrapped chocolate bar. 'You can't say no to chocolate.'
'Thank you.'
'So, what's your name?'
'Tulsi.' I put the chocolate in my pocket.
'Well, that sounds fancy. Does it mean anything?'
'It's a kind of holy leaf.'

She Came to Stay

'That's just perfect,' she said as she patted me on my head. 'I think I'll call you Holy Leaf.' She repeated the words to herself like a chant.

'Mamoni,' I said, 'should we show Miss Ruby to her room?'

Ruby laughed.

'Did I say something wrong?'

'Don't call me Miss Ruby. I'm not some old school mistress, Holy Leaf. Just Ruby will do.'

I could feel my cheeks turning red.

We showed Ruby to her room in the attic just above my room and I put the case on the wooden chair that was tucked beneath the eaves.

'That's my guitar,' she said. 'Ever heard of the Beatles?'

'Kind of,' I said.

'I can teach you a few strings if you hang out with me, Holy Leaf.'

The very idea of learning to play the guitar thrilled me. I liked her already.

Mamoni showed Ruby a cupboard in the bathroom on the first floor where the fresh linen and towels were kept, and then we took our new guest on a tour of the house. I did most of the talking and Mamoni added the odd piece of information, often stopping to ask me in Bengali for help translating. She smiled at Ruby a lot even though I knew she struggled to understand her accent and what exactly she was saying.

'We are eating dinner in kitchen,' Mamoni said as she showed Ruby the kitchen and that's when I noticed how shabby the house was, the floor with its chipped red tiles and the stained worktops.

'Where is Mr. Basu?' asked Ruby.

'My husband coming home every evening.'

I was embarrassed for Mamoni. 'She means, he's usually back home by seven or eight every night,' I said, but Ruby had already left the kitchen and moved to the lounge.

We followed her.

Baba came home from work at eight and went straight to the kitchen.

Ruby didn't join us for a meal that night as she'd eaten a heavy lunch and so Baba and Mamoni and I ate alone.

'I hope you haven't been making a nuisance of yourself to our new lodger?' Baba said as he ate the rice and fish, gravy trickling through his fingers. I could tell from the way Mamoni clattered the pots on the cooker that she wasn't pleased by his comment. I didn't want them to start another row, not with Ruby upstairs.

'She has a guitar, Baba,' I said. 'Can I have one too?'

He didn't answer.

'Ruby said she can teach me how to play.' Baba looked at Mamoni, who stood rigidly at the sink scouring an oven dish.

'We've talked about this, Tulsi. We cannot afford a guitar at the moment, let alone music lessons.'

'Things were so different in Bhawanipur,' Mamoni said quietly to herself and began to slap a cloth randomly on the kitchen counter.

'What are you mumbling about Ketaki?'

When she turned around, Mamoni was flushed and she didn't look straight at Baba.

'Who'd have thought we'd have to keep a paying stranger to make ends meet?' She twisted the end of her sari between her fingers.

I shouldn't have mentioned the guitar.

I rinsed my plate at the sink, tried to shut out their voices and hummed the tune to 'All things Bright and Beautiful' that I'd learnt at assembly that morning.

It was nearly nine o'clock when Ruby came down from the attic. Baba stood to greet her and even standing as tall as he could, with his neck stretched and his chin jutting forward, he barely reached her shoulders.

'Very nice to meet you Mr. Basu,' said Ruby. She put out her hand, but grains of yellow rice stuck to the side of Baba's palm and so he just waved his hand towards the chair opposite him.

'Please sit down,' he said.

She sat and tucked one leg beneath her and the other one up so her chin rested on her knee and spoke to Baba about the rent.

'This month's rent in advance,' she said, and put an envelope next to his empty plate.

Baba nodded. He put the envelope in his pocket and didn't say thank you.

When I got into bed that night, I heard the floorboards creak above and Ruby strumming her guitar. I smiled as the music dulled the bitter and raised voices coming from my parents' bedroom.

I began to spend a lot of time with Ruby. When I got home from school I'd race up to her room where I'd find her sprawled on her bed. She'd jump up when she saw me and we'd muck around with the guitar until Mamoni called us down for dinner. In those early days, the atmosphere at home seemed to lift a little bit as if everything had just had a spring clean. Even Baba sounded more cheerful when Ruby was around.

One evening, just before dinner, I snuck into Ruby's attic room which was dark except for a square shaft of brightness from the skylight. Ruby had gone out to her job as a barmaid at the Fox and Duck on the corner of our street. Mamoni was cooking dinner. I knew I shouldn't have been there but I wanted to have a quick strum on the guitar. Surely Ruby wouldn't mind my being there when she was out. She'd told me I could borrow the guitar whenever I felt like it.

On her nightstand were books and a pot with her beads and earrings. I tried a pair of earrings on in front of the mirror and blinked to see myself changed then sat on her bed and bounced up and down, smoothed out the creases on her duvet cover and, as I ran my fingers across her pillowcase, I felt something hard beneath my palm. It was a square ruby earring.

I sat with the earring for a while, conscious of the sound of my own breathing. Then I put it back where I'd found it and went downstairs to my own room. My heart beat an uneven rhythm in my chest.

The earring belonged to Mamoni.

It was an afternoon in late-October, and Ruby had been with us for almost a month. I sat at the kitchen table doing my math's homework as Mamoni cooked dinner. Ruby was home as she usually was in the afternoons and sat next to me. Her clothes smelt of stale cigarette smoke and there were bags under her eyes. Her hair was pulled back into a tightly wound knot and I could see the green flecks in her irises. I was usually asleep when Ruby came home and she was hardly ever up in the mornings when I left for school, so this was the only time I saw her. Ever since I'd found Mamoni's earing under Ruby's pillow I'd become awkward when I was around both of them. I knew she was alone with Mamoni for most of the day, I wondered what they said to each other, what they did.

Ruby looked into my school notebook.

'Fractions? I used to love doing sums,' she said. 'Are you good at fractions, Holy Leaf?'

'Tulsi does not like her mathematics subject,' Mamoni said. 'It is not her favourite.'

'That doesn't look right,' Ruby said, and pointed to a fraction that I'd been working on for a while now.

There was a crack and splutter of spices thrown in a hot pan and soon the room was smoky with the aroma of cardamom and roasted cumin.

'What are you making today, Kets?' asked Ruby. She cupped her mug of tea. I noticed how slim and tapered her fingers were, the nails short and chipped at the edges. She chewed her nails.

When had she shortened Mamoni's name to Kets? The familiarity of this irked me and it bothered me even more when Ruby got up to look over Mamoni's shoulder and asked to help with the cooking.

'Ruby, first you learning all spices before you cooking Bengali food,' said Mamoni as she threw chopped spinach into the pan.

'Okay then, teach me, Kets.' Ruby turned and winked at me. 'I'm pretty sure I know more than you think. Here, let me have a look at your spice tin.'

Ruby brought the round steel spice tin to the table and put it next to my notebooks. I moved out of the way. She left me no choice.

'Right, let's start with this yellow stuff,' said Ruby. She was enjoying this too much. 'Turmeric?'

Ruby brought the pot of turmeric close to her face and sniffed. Her nose caught a speck of yellow powder.

'Oh, na, na. Be careful it is giving stains,' said Mamoni.

This was turning into a game, Ruby sniffing and tasting and trying to guess what each spice was and Mamoni nodding or shaking her head and placing whole spices onto Ruby's tongue.

I gathered up my notebooks and went upstairs to my room.

Later that week there was a power cut. Ruby was at work and I was helping Mamoni dry the dishes after dinner.

'This is the second time this week,' Baba said from the sudden darkness at the table.

'Ketaki, Tulsi, stay where you are, don't move until I've found a candle.'

I didn't mind the dark. I watched my parents fuss at lighting the candles, making sure I wasn't too close to the flames.

'Watch your hair Tulsi,' Mamoni said as we made our way down the hallway to the living room, each of us carrying a candle. Our shadows danced on the yellow papered walls. We huddled round the coffee table and Baba brought his paper and read out snippets of news.

The darkness and candlelight seemed to kindle a rare intimacy, and it comforted me to hear my parents speak to each other softly, their breath mingling over the trembling flames. I was disappointed when the lights came back on and in a matter of minutes, Mamoni and Baba became distant and awkward again.

'Time for bed now Tulsi,' Baba said and patted my cheek. He went to his armchair with his newspaper and Mamoni blew out the candles and went back to the kitchen.

In November, Ruby wanted to teach Mamoni to drive.

'Think of the freedom, Kets,' she said. 'All those wonderful drives you could take. And you could drive Tulsi to school.'

She Came to Stay

I said nothing. I didn't want to be drawn into Ruby's scheme.

'I'll ask Samir,' said Mamoni. She was worried about asking Baba for permission.

'He promised he would teach me driving after we married but he has not had time to do this.'

I'd become aware of the growing closeness between Ruby and Mamoni, the way Ruby rested her hand on Mamoni's shoulder when she was cooking and once I saw her kissing the top of Mamoni's head as she podded a bowl of peas. I'd also seen them hugging.

Mamoni was often late picking me up from school and when she came she looked flushed and happy. I smelt Ruby's cigarettes on Mamoni's sari and in her hair and knew she'd spent the day with her new friend.

Maybe Mamoni found Ruby more interesting than me and I should've been happy that she had someone to talk to during the day, but I wasn't. Instead, I started mimicking Ruby and smothered Mamoni with kisses or hugs whenever Ruby was around.

Mamoni finally asked Baba about taking lessons.

'I don't think so,' said Baba. 'The car is not insured and I do not approve of taking lessons from Ruby. It's madness.'

'But Ruby is a good driver,' said Mamoni, 'and the car is just lying there all week.'

Baba shook his head and brought his newspaper up in front of his face. The conversation ended.

On Monday, after school, Ruby was waiting next to our car, a small green Fiat, with a cushion in her hands. I guessed that Mamoni had lessons with Ruby when Baba and I were out.

'Right, today is the day you show Holy Leaf what you've learnt so far.' She grinned and propped Mamoni into the driving seat. I sat in the back, behind Ruby, and the lesson began.

Ruby sat tall in the seat, her head almost touching the roof, her long legs crossed sideways. She started the car by leaning over Mamoni's lap to turn the key. The car shivered.

'Come on then, Kets, you can do this. Show us what a good driver you already are.'

'You keep talking Ruby, please,' Mamoni said. 'This is just my third lesson with you.'

We crept out onto the open road, Mamoni drove slowly. As she approached each crossing or a traffic light. Ruby told her what to do, helping her with the controls, the gear shift and even put her foot on the brakes a couple of times. There was a lot of cranking and changing of gears. Cars beeped going past. Mamoni stared straight ahead and, a few miles from the house, near the big Tesco, without warning, she started going faster and swerved between lanes.

I said nothing, not one word. Mamoni leant forward in her seat as she drove up a steep road. She was probably afraid the car would roll backwards and I was scared too, but didn't say so, just gripped the passenger-seat headrest. When we reached the top of the steep hill, Mamoni leaned back, laughing as she exhaled.

'That wasn't so bad was it?' said Ruby. 'You're doing so great.'

Then Ruby brushed a loose strand of hair from Mamoni's face, her finger lingering on Mamoni's bare neck.

I turned away.

For a while I stared out the window, afraid of the passing trucks on Selhurst Road. The steep verges of the Downs seemed to close in on both sides. I wanted Mamoni to slow down, but she didn't. Mamoni kept on pressing the accelerator and the car hit a bollard at the bottom of the hill. I flew between the front seats, my chin hitting the dashboard. For a moment everything was still and quiet until the horn began to wail and Mamoni sobbed.

Ruby dragged me out of the car. The front of my shirt was soaked with the blood dripping from my chin.

Ruby told me to sit on the curb and tilt my head back, all the time holding a rag to my face. The bonnet of the car was mangled, the windscreen cracked and there was splintered glass on the road from the smashed headlamps.

I don't know who called the ambulance but before I knew it, I was in the emergency room, lying on a gurney, getting stitches in my chin. Baba rushed from work to the hospital. He spoke to the doctor in a loud voice and signed the forms and said nothing to either Ruby or Mamoni. Mamoni's sari was hitched messily above her ankles and her hair was strewn wildly across her shoulders.

'She'll be fine, it's just a small cut,' Ruby said. She stood next to Baba but he ignored her and put his arm across my shoulders and steered me ahead to the taxi that brought us home to Maple Drive.

The next day, when I got home from school I guessed from Mamoni's pursed lips and puffy eyes that Ruby was gone. We sat in the kitchen and sipped tea in silence. It got late and the room drew close to darkness. Mamoni didn't get up to switch on the lights. I wanted to say something to her but my words seemed to sink into my throat.

When Baba came home from work, she got up, put his food on the table then locked herself in her bedroom. I wished they'd argue but they didn't say a single word except when Baba told me to do my homework.

I waited till Baba sat with his paper in the front room then I crept up to the attic. None of the lights worked and the air stank of cigarettes. A stray shard of light from the window highlighted the tired wallpaper, the stained wood on the dresser. I sat on the naked mattress and noticed Ruby's guitar-case leaning against the wall.

How could she have forgotten?

I opened the door to let in some light from the landing, then lifted the case onto the bed and unsnapped the clasps. A piece of tightly folded paper fell out.

'Holy Leaf. This guitar is for you. I won't be needing it anymore.'

Next morning, before Baba woke, before Mamoni started making his breakfast, I left early for school, and I walked alone.

ALISTAIR DANIEL

The Box

The box was bigger than the man was expecting: big enough to hold a car seat, or a crib for a one-year-old child. As promised, there were no markings on the outside, just a set of arrows indicating the right way up and a sticker that read 'Private & Personal: To Be Opened By Addressee Only'.

'Alright pal,' said the DPD man.

The man signed the little electronic tablet with a scrawl that did not resemble his name, and the DPD man waddled back to his van, whistling 'Life on Mars'.

The man carried the box upstairs. It felt light – no more than six or seven pounds. He could not decide where to put it so he set it down on the landing and went to fetch a knife. The knives were not where they were supposed to be, in the wooden block in the kitchen, so he took a pair of scissors from the cutlery drawer and hurried back up the stairs and cut through the tape – even though he was not the addressee – carefully, so as not to damage the contents. Inside he found an A4 information folder, two padded envelopes packed with boxes of pills, a polythene bag full of syringes and needles and a plastic sharps bin with 'DANGER' printed on the side. He opened the folder and read through the information, then he took out the rest of the contents and laid them on the carpet at the top of the stairs, checking them off against the delivery note one by one:

7 x Cetrotide 0.25mg injection
6 x Merional 75iu (packs of 10 vials)
1 x Gonasi 5000iu/1ml
63 x Norethisterone 5mg tablets
32 x Cyclogest (400mg) pessaries
1 x Sharps Bin

When he'd finished he fetched the hook from the study and opened the hatch on the landing. He dragged the ladder to the floor and climbed into the loft with the box tucked under one arm. The loft was hot, and the box was not supposed to be hot, so he climbed back down and put the ladder away and closed the hatch. He carried the box to the spare room – which was undecorated – and set it down on the bed. Then he returned to his study. He opened an email from his client – the director of a classical music festival – and read the brief. He clicked on some links and listened for a while. Then he wrote:

Composed in a burst of creativity, Handel's Messiah *made its debut at the Great Music Hall in Dublin on 13 April 1742. The evening was a triumph (one critic called it 'the finest composition of musick that ever was heard'), yet for the London premiere Handel made numerous revisions. The original version – if not quite lost – was rarely heard again.*

For the closing event in this year's festival, Berlin's renowned Handel Camerata joins forces with our very own Festival Chorus to present the original version of the Messiah. *Performed in the magnificent surroundings of St Anne's, this stunning finale is a wonderful opportunity to discover the great composer's masterpiece as its very first audience would have heard it.*

* * *

In the evening the woman came home from a sales conference in Spain. She stood in the doorway of the spare room and looked at the box.

'Jesus,' she said.

'I know,' said the man.

* * *

It had been the man's idea to order the box.

As he got older he'd been visited by strange new urges. The urge to make something and leave it behind. The urge to pass on what he'd learned. Why agriculture developed in the Fertile Crescent. Why house music was always in a minor key. Why the best chance of life in the Solar System – outside of Earth – was on Mars. He imagined buying a blackboard and drawing on it when learning opportunities arose. He imagined decorating the spare room with a poster of the periodic table, with a globe that lit up from inside, with ceiling stars that glowed in the dark. He spent a lot of time imagining these things.

The woman was less keen than the man. When he mentioned it she flushed at the neck and her breathing turned shallow and fast. She liked her sister's children and enjoyed their company for up to an hour, but she had never felt any urges, she told him, educational or otherwise. Her career – she worked for a company that made diving cylinders – was going well. But she agreed they would try.

At first their efforts were haphazard. They had sex when they felt like it and not when they did not. They kept no record of these attempts. It would happen when it would happen. But nothing happened.

After a year the man said they needed to take it more seriously. He bought a twelve-pack of boxers, took cold baths and drank expensive powdered sachets full of vitamins and zinc. He started jogging and cut down on alcohol. His body mass index went down to 24.

The woman tried to take it more seriously, but she found it harder than the man. She forgot to take her folic acid, struggled to keep track of her cycle and drank a glass of wine every night. Her work demanded long hours and frequent trips abroad, and when she did come home she was often too exhausted for sex.

When nothing continued to occur the man bought ovulation kits and began to keep a record of the woman's cycle in a leather-bound journal. Every day, for a week every month, the woman urinated onto a stick. The man made a playlist of music he thought she ought to enjoy – some Bowie but mostly Handel's *Messiah* – and on the optimal days they had sex. Afterwards the woman went into the bathroom and stayed there a long time.

The man drove the woman to baby showers and christenings. He brought gender-neutral T-shirts and picture books with empowering messages and bibs that read 'Give Peas a Chance'. At weekends he invited friends with young children to stay. The friends all told the woman about the transformative experience they were having. The children screamed and were sick in the night.

The woman got a promotion. The frequency of her business trips increased.

After two years their GP referred them for tests. The woman had X-Rays and cervical swabs and an ultrasound probe inserted into her vagina. The man provided a semen sample. His sperm had low motility. The woman was clinically geriatric. She was entitled to one free round, the consultant advised them, but only until her next birthday, which was coming up in three weeks. The box was by far their best chance. It had to be now.

* * *

At the hospital they took two seats in the waiting room: a clean white space with sofas and coffee tables that was trying hard to feel like a café. The couples around them spoke in whispers or looked at their phones. The woman took a quarterly sales report out of her bag and clicked the top of her pen. The man stared at a TV mounted on the wall. The screen was divided in two. The smaller section explained the process of embryo transfer through a slideshow of cheerful cartoons. The main section was showing *Sky News*. George III was now thought to have been bipolar. Pictures sent back by NASA's *Romulus* probe revealed a body of liquid water lying just beneath the surface of Mars.

The box sat on the table in front of them like a marrow they had entered for a prize.

The nurse called them: a woman in her fifties with dyed black hair. Her manner was brisk but not unpleasant. She opened the box and took out the drugs. She showed the woman how to flick the neck of the little ampoule so the solvent dropped to the bottom of the chamber, how to use the snapper to break the ampoule's neck, how to squirt the solvent into the powder and draw the solution back into the syringe, how to flick the syringe to send the air bubbles to the top, how to push the air out of the needle until the solution beaded at the tip, where in the stomach to inject. She must begin on Tuesday, the nurse said.

The man found it extraordinary that a handful of chemicals could create conditions receptive to life, and said so.

'We're all chemicals, love,' said the nurse. She turned to the woman. 'Do you want to give it a go?'

The woman flinched and shook her head.

They returned to the car. The man laid the box on the back seat, but he noticed the woman staring at him. Her neck was turning red. He retrieved the box and put it in the boot.

* * *

On Tuesday the woman didn't come home.

That afternoon the man had washed his hands carefully and taken out all the chemicals and tools. He'd attached a long green needle to a syringe and opened a box of Merional and taken out the ampoule and vial and laid everything on a square of kitchen towel on the table beside the spare bed. Then he'd waited. When the woman did not appear the man left a message on her phone and went into the kitchen. He made a goat's cheese tart, though it was difficult without any knives, and after each preparation stage he stopped and tried to call, but there was no reply. By the time the tart was ready he no longer felt hungry so he left it in the oven to keep warm. He went upstairs and stood in the spare room with his nails digging into his palms. After a while he sat down on the bed and began to read the list of side effects in the leaflet that came with each pack: diarrhoea, stomach pain, vomiting, ovarian cysts. Eventually his phone rang. It was a friend. The woman was in hospital – a different one, for people who were injured and sick. The man grabbed his jacket and left.

He found her in the casualty ward, talking to the friend. She had seven stitches in her forehead and a crimson swelling under one eye. She'd left work on time, she said, but found herself struggling for air. Then she blacked out and when she came to she was lying in the street. It was nothing. A panic attack, that was all.

When they got home the man helped the woman into bed. He kissed her on the forehead, just over the wound, then he went into the spare room and dropped the syringe into the sharps bin and threw the chemicals into the box. He lay down on the bed, with the box beside him, and stared at the whitewashed, starless ceiling. In the middle of the night he got up and put the box in the loft.

* * *

The receptionist answered at the third ring.

'Sospita?'

'Hi,' said the man. 'We got a delivery the other week, but we don't need it anymore.'

'Oh,' said the receptionist. 'Congratulations!'

There was a pause. 'What should I do with the box?' said the man, finally.

'Give it to the hospital next time you're in there, love,' said the receptionist. 'They'll get rid of it for you.'

The man hung up and returned to his desk. He read an email from the festival director, then he opened the draft. *'This may be your only chance,'* he wrote, *'to hear Handel's original masterpiece performed by one of the world's greatest ensembles amid the Gothic splendour of St Anne's.'*

The man looked at the screen for a while, then he got up and walked across the landing. He opened the hatch and pulled the ladder down and climbed into the loft. Inside it was warm and dark. The box was sitting in a corner beside a support beam. He reached into it and pulled out all the packages and laid them on the floor in neat rows. When the box was empty he got down on all fours and tried to back into it, but he could only fit one leg inside. He left it there and rolled onto his side. He reached for a syringe and opened a box of Merional and prepared the solution, snapping the ampoule's neck with one hand. He pushed the plunger until the solution beaded on the needle's tip. Lifting his T-shirt, he aimed the syringe at his stomach, just below the navel, and thrust the needle inside.

ALEX DAWES

The Note

The country was not yet in flames. Dead kids on college campuses, running battles in the streets, soldiers hurling medals at the White House; all this waited, rage bubbling under the surface, battle-lines drawn and hardening each day, a conflict creeping, building, growing and soon, ready to explode.

But not yet. It was still 1965, the opening skirmishes. Blake was only distantly aware of any of this, mostly interested in himself, the outside world an unwelcome intrusion, and he woke to it annoyed on a cold November morning choked white with snow, a dirty yellow cab honking outside of his window, South Williamsburg, New York.

Was it morning? He checked his bedside clock and saw blurred hands merging somewhere near the top. Lunchtime. His mouth was full of ash; bitter, dry, hot. He had been smoking again. Blake sat up. No chance of going back to sleep. The cab outside's honking had started in his dreams and followed him into the waking world, and now he was trapped in dreadful reality, thirsty and dirty. *Well that's it*, Blake thought turning out of bed, bare feet burning against the cold linoleum floor.

'Janice?' he called. Nothing. He was alone. A cold winter sun filled the apartment showing more than Blake wanted; dishes swimming in shiny water thick with grease in the kitchenette, piles of clothes heaped on furniture, a black, oozing banana watching him from a table. This was how he lived. Neither he nor Janice cleaned unless absolutely necessary, until the mess threatened disease and vermin, and then it became a war, scorched earth, sheets stripped from the bed and thrown away, walls and floors scrubbed white.

'Janice?' Still nothing. He kicked a sock across the apartment hoping Janice might be underneath, but no.

Don't go steady with someone like you, his Mom had always said. And she'd been right; he and Janice were bad for each other, objectively; you could measure it by the rising ashtrays and overflowing sink. Though they were not dirty people in themselves. Not at all. In fact, quite glamorous, in their way. Janice had something of Audrey Hepburn in the way she held her neck, an innocent, yet knowing sheen in her eyes and jet-black, immaculate hair. Blake, also dark, Italian and some Greek in his blood bubbling to the surface in sharp, satanic features, a deep voice with well-hit vowels, so you listened whenever he spoke. And when he smiled, he seemed evil, a supervillain, with eyebrows that could cut glass, so you could not look away. Together, Janice and Blake, in the right light, in the right mood, they could capture a room, they were royalty.

But neither could empty a bin.

'Janice?' She was out, definitely out, maybe shopping, maybe at Chock full O' Nuts swirling coffee. 'I want coffee,' Blake said mournfully to the empty apartment, but no one brought him any.

Blake padded across the floor and found the kitchenette empty, no coffee, and in the corner of his eye in the reflection of a cracked window saw fresh mail on a round table propped up against a vase. A single flower in the vase sagged in brown water, and with the mail underneath, it looked to Blake's sleep clouded mind like an absurd question mark.

He walked over. A letter for him was among the others. Something stirred in Blake's gut; electricity, excitement, an unpleasant sickness. It was from Gordon Hirsh. Blake could tell by the unsteady typeset, smeared letters at war with each other. He'd received letters, all rejections, half a dozen or so, from Gordon's magazine already, which published short stories and poetry. He knew the typeset well; he waited for it, he dreaded it.

So here it is. Blake's last story had been his best, so he thought. Maybe this was it. He looked at the envelope and turned it carefully, feeling its weight in his hand. Not much to it. Just a sliver of paper folded up inside another sliver of paper, and on the paper inside the other paper, who knew: a yes or a no. Acceptance with a cheque at three cents a word rounded down to the nearest dollar, or a thanks but no thanks. And sometimes, something else. A *note*, handwritten by Gordon himself. This most of all. Gordon only wrote notes for the work he really liked, for stories that burned with promise but were not quite *there*, and his notes were famed for their far-reaching, supernatural insight. A note could change everything about you, make you see yourself in a new light, change the way you did everything. Like a map to buried treasure or a clue to finding yourself.

Now or never, thought Blake. He opened the envelope casually, whistling, working his thumb under the flap, carefully tearing away at the adhesive, all the while his heart thundering in his chest.

This could be it, Blake thought as his thumb turned and worked. *The moment everything changes. Right now, a nobody. After, a somebody. Years from now I'll be able to say: this is where it started, this moment, this letter, this...* The inner monologue stopped. Blake's thumb was turning in empty space. The envelope was open; it was done. He looked down and saw folded paper within. A tremor went through his heart. *Maybe it's like*

The Note

Schrodinger's cat, Blake thought, *neither dead nor alive until you look at it.* It gave Blake pause. Looking would give him the answer; he wasn't sure he wanted it, it had never been a good answer before.

Blake's hands decided for themselves. Out came the letter, folded in half, opened by trembling fingers. He saw nothing. Blake couldn't make sense of it; too much blood and adrenaline throbbing in his head. He tried to breathe. *Look at it.* A scrawl of words, handwritten. Not a simple yes or no. *The other one.* Blake sat down, pushing empty packets and cartons onto the floor from a chair. *When will we finally clean this disgusting apartment?* A stray thought asked. *Not for a few weeks.* He and Janice weren't quite there yet, still in a desperate race to the bottom until one of them could stand the mess no more.

The note, Blake remembered. But it still didn't make sense. Two sentences? Three sentences. All tangled together. Punctuation and letters vomited onto the page. Gordon wrote like a doctor, a million times worse. He didn't even try to make sense. Blake slammed the note aside. He stared into space and thought of coffee and cigarettes.

'Janice?' he called. *Where's she going to be, in the closet? Under the bed? You know she's out.* Blake sighed. He looked back at the note, still didn't understand it, put it aside once more.

Noise came from outside, as if conjured up by Blake's mind: it was Janice on the stairs. He could tell by the footsteps, he knew her climpty-clop approach, and more, that she had shopping. The footsteps were different with her hands full. An extra clop in the climpty. Janice rattled at the door and a few seconds later came in backwards, a brown paper shopping bag bulging with flowers and food. *She's always buying flowers, and they're always dying,* Blake thought annoyed.

'There's my sleeping beauty,' Janice said. She walked past Blake and put the shopping to rest on the table. A packet of Frankfurter sausages wrapped in cellophane slid out of the bag, but Blake couldn't think about eating, his stomach twisting into knots.

The note was still in his hand, and Janice darted a look at it. 'What's that?'

'A note from Gordon Hirsh.'

Janice gasped. Two years of writing and this was the first thing Blake had to show for it. 'A note?'

Blake nodded gravely. 'A note.'

'What does it say?'

He handed it to her. 'Well, I think you should see for yourself.'

Janice did not look at the note right away; first she sat down, glasses emerging from a small pink case and afterwards the case closed with a snap, the glasses then placed carefully on her face, then a deep breath, and finally she opened the note.

'I can't read it,' she said. Of course. Janice was always blunt. She was a bad-tempered woman when you got down to it, and she only had time for the truth. 'What does it say?' she asked Blake.

'I don't know,' he shrugged. 'I was hoping you would.'

They made a joint effort. The note was turned and considered from several angles, in the sunlight by a window, on its side under a lamp, but no headway was made.

Janice pointed at a curling letter, probably capitalised, halfway into the second sentence. 'I think that says France,' she said.

Blake sighed. 'Why the fuck would Gordon talk about France, Janice?'

Janice blinked back her anger. On another day she would tear the flesh from Blake's bones for that, but today she gave him a pass. 'Why don't you go and see Jan?' she asked in a restrained voice. 'He's good at this kind of thing.'

Well, not exactly, Blake thought. But Jan was *someone else*, another set of eyes. 'Fine,' said Blake.

He threw on a coat and flew down two flights of stairs, into the New York winter. Deep snow muddy with footprints was piled high on the sidewalk and thin clouds of vapour dissipated from pale faces in the midmorning sun, with more snow on the road blasted brown by exhaust and smashed into dense submission by heavy tyres. The whole world was dirty white, grey and yellow, like grubby teeth.

Jan had a bar, or managed one (it was never really clear), four blocks away, just a quick jaunt over two crosswalks and around a corner. Blake moved quickly towards it, the note flapping in his hand like Charlie's golden ticket, anxiety needling away at him.

But hadn't this been the plan? Yes. There was always going to be letters and rejections. The *then* before the *now*. Move to New York, make friends with the writers and the English majors in the East Village, and someone's father would be in publishing or an agent, and they'd get Blake *in*. He'd make it. So easy from the safety of his mind, but it had never occurred to Blake he might not have anything interesting to say, or worse, that he might not have the talent to say anything well enough for anyone to listen. This more than anything. Good ideas; but they never made it onto paper with any weight. His dialogue stank. Everything was telegraphed. People just said what they thought. No subtext. How do you write two people talking in a room? How did it start? Should someone come into the room first? Should they already be there? Blake didn't know two years ago, and he still didn't know now.

The Note

Blake danced along the sidewalk through thickening crowds. A man walking with an open newspaper thrust a headline in Blake's direction which said: *While Brave Men Die: The Riddle of Vietnam.*

The war. Blake had thought about writing about it. But what did he know? Blake hadn't volunteered. He was too smart and too afraid for that. He had nothing to say, only what he read in the papers and what his beatnik friends in Chelsea told him to think. Blake hadn't melted any children with napalm or taken LSD or mescaline or psilocybin mushrooms in the jungle, and he hadn't lived in the trees and become strange and primitive and come home a stranger and been rejected by his wife. He was fundamentally tamed and passive, too afraid of risk and losing what little he had to try something new, and so he had nothing worth saying. And before him lay a dark road with only one obvious end.

Law school.

It was really quite pathetic; he saw himself a failure. And all the while his typewriter sat and watched, clank, clank, clank as Blake bashed away at the keys, nothing of note coming out from those black, rubbery rollers. The only impact he was going to have with the damn thing was hurling it out of the window from two floors up so it smashed some poor passer-by's brains in. And it would – his typewriter was heavy, damn heavy, and Blake had thought about it, chucking it through the glass and seeing the chaos below; blood and bone in the snow. *At least I did something*, he'd be able to say.

But now the note. The mysterious, untouchable, elusive note; the final piece of the puzzle, except of course, Blake couldn't read it.

What the fuck is written on this fucking note?

He was at Jan's, and he pounded on the door. It was a heavy door, and Jan was probably asleep, so it needed an extra hard pounding, which Blake did, enjoying the hard satisfaction of his fist against the wood. Thud, thud, thud.

Jan arrived more quickly than Blake expected, throwing open the door so fast Blake's final thud hit empty air, undoing the catharsis of all that smashing.

'Blake!' Jan bellowed obnoxiously into the street. He was still in his barman's uniform which was stained and somewhat dishevelled, a vague smell of booze around him, sweet and chemical. 'Wonderful. So glad you're here. I have huge news! Huge!' Jan turned back towards the darkness of the bar, and Blake followed him inside.

'*I* have huge news,' Blake corrected.

Jan closed the door behind them and pulled up a blind letting in the sun. The light caught a mirror near the back of the room, and Blake turned to avoid its glimmer. He had been avoiding his own reflection for some time now, not liking the stinking bag of failure he saw staring back. Janice cut his hair, so he didn't need to go to the barber, and the rest was just a simple matter of averting his eyes now and then. Only on Halloween a few weeks ago had he really stared at his own reflection, and only then on the orders of Janice, with her dressed as a witch with a long green nose, and him a pale ghost complete with white makeup, and he'd thought, while staring at his own stupid, hateful face, *you really are a ghoul, aren't you?*

'We can *both* have huge news,' Jan said happily sliding behind the bar.

Blake sat on a barstool with the note in his hand. He looked around and thought the place seemed strangely vulnerable and empty in the daytime, as if all the patrons who came to drink and smoke in booths or propped up against the bar actually held the place up, and without them now the roof might fall in.

'I have a note,' Blake said.

'Great,' answered Jan, not listening. He found two glasses and filled them with something brown and boozy and half translucent and dropped in a few ice cubes with quick hands and a shiny set of tongs. The sound of ice against glass brought out a thirst in Blake, and he took a swig from the freshly poured brown stuff and felt a warm, dreamy sensation burn down his throat.

'What's your big news?' Blake asked.

'I just fucked Ruth Flinders.'

Blake tried to place her in his mind. 'Surely you mean Ruth Clark?'

Jan shook his head. 'Ruth *Flinders*.' He hit the *Flinders* hard, rolling each syllable, making it last.

'Ruth Flinders,' Blake repeated. It was quite a coup. Ruth Flinders was far out of Jan's league, but then, women *did* seem to like Jan. He was tall and rangy and filled the room with his voice, but he also had a strange face. It was difficult to say exactly what made Jan's face strange, but it was generally agreed by all (Jan included) that his face *was* strange. And yet, women liked him.

'What happened?' Blake asked. Suddenly the note seemed unimportant, and Blake let it creep back into the safety of his pocket.

'She just stuck around after closing. Next thing I know,' Jan made a vulgar gesture with his hands, 'right here on the bar.'

Blake lifted his resting arms from the place Jan pointed. 'I hope you cleaned it afterwards.' Blake was something of a germ-freak, even though he was happy to wallow in his own and Janice's filth for months on end. But that was Blake's dirt, and he was fine with it.

Jan glugged down the last of his drink. 'So what's your news?'

The Note

Blake reached into his pocket. 'I got a note from Gordon Hirsh.'

'Seriously?' Jan wiped his mouth with the back of his hand. 'What a day this has been for both of us. What did the note say?'

'No idea, you read it.'

Jan stared. 'My friend, I do not have a clue. It's a mystery.' And yet he kept the note, fingering and pawing at it, holding it up to the light. Blake suddenly became worried that Jan might keep the note as a trophy alongside Ruth Flinders and no one would remember Blake got it, except Blake. Jan, perhaps catching this thought, gave Blake back the note. 'We should ask him,' Jan said.

'Gordon Hirsh?'

'Why not? He gave you the note. Just ask.'

Just ask. Blake vaguely recalled Janice yelling something like this as he left the apartment, but then it had seemed ridiculous. Now out of Jan's mouth, the idea made sense.

'He might not let me in,' Blake said. Gordon was famously difficult and eccentric, and in the silence he and Jan considered this the phone rang loudly in the cavern of the empty bar. Jan leaned over and picked it up with one of his long arms.

'Janice!' Jan said. Blake heard Janice speak on the other side of the phone, and Jan listening. Those two always listened to each other, they liked to gang up on Blake in that friendly, unbearable way only friends who knew you well could. 'That's what *I* said,' Jan said. 'What a great idea. We'll see you there!' He slammed the phone down and turned triumphantly towards Blake. 'We're going to see Gordon Hirsh to ask about this note.'

'Now?'

'Now!'

They fell out of the bar into a darkening afternoon. Another walk in the cold, this time to Gordon's magazine, *The South Street Witness*. The city busied itself around them, disinterested in their small drama, men in hats and suits, square cars and bright signs, boys shouting and hurling snowballs, women from windows screaming down at them, and more, the city unfolding and disappearing at each turned corner.

'Will Gordon see us?' Blake asked as they waited at a crosswalk.

'Janice has a girlfriend at the office there who can get us in. She said she only remembered after you left.' That, or she decided to withhold the information in small revenge for Blake's short temper. *That's just the kind of thing she'd do,* Blake thought. *Let me suffer to teach me a lesson.*

'There she is,' Jan said.

It was Janice waiting on a corner wrapped in a storm coat and wearing green pumps and a red fedora hat, the only clothes she could find lying around Blake guessed, standing there in the snow looking beautiful and absurd.

'Got another one of those?' Blake asked about the cigarette hanging from her mouth.

'Get your own, it's my last one.'

'Is this it?' Jan asked about the office above.

'It used to have a sign,' Janice said.

They all stood there a minute, huddled outside and waiting for someone to do something.

'Well?' asked Blake.

'Let me finish,' Janice said about her cigarette. She didn't smoke often, only when she was nervous or about to perform a big set with her band. She was a great singer with a thick, smoky voice, but she mostly played the trumpet on stage, because there were a thousand beautiful women in New York who could sing but only one who could play the trumpet, and that was Janice.

She crushed her cigarette under the ball of her foot. 'Let's do this,' she said.

They pushed open the door into a dark corridor and saw stairs leading upwards. It was warm and close in there, an old heater roasting in the space, so by the time he reached the top, Blake felt woozy with heat and darkness.

'Here it is,' Janice said.

After all that, and it was just a small and tattered office with splintering desks and crooked chairs that might have been recovered from a flea market, with a few green lamps scattered around and another smaller office in a corner. *That's where Gordon Hirsh works,* Blake thought. But right now the office was empty, as was the rest of the place, except for a secretary a few steps away behind another battered desk.

'Oh,' said Janice, and her face swam with panic. Blake could tell right away this wasn't the secretary Janice had been expecting; it was someone else; an old woman with a sour, expressionless face, her hair and skin all grey so that she looked like a fuzzy rock.

'Can I help you three sweeties?' the secretary asked.

No one answered. They had fallen at the first hurdle, and the whole adventure was destined to fail. Blake was surprised to feel a wash of cold relief in his belly at this; he'd decided on the way up he didn't want to know what was on the note after all. It could only be the truth, and the truth about Blake wasn't something Blake wanted, it turned out.

'Sure, you can help,' said Janice. Resolve hardened in her face; she was going to do this anyway. She marched over from the door towards the

The Note

secretary with Blake and Jan in her wake. 'We're here to see Gordon Hirsh,' she said flatly.

Evil satisfaction spread across the secretary's face. 'Gordon doesn't see visitors,' she said, spitting out the words like an incantation or a chant. *Gordon doesn't see visitors, Gordon doesn't see visitors.*

She lives for this shit, thought Blake. *Turning people away, shredding their dreams.*

'We have an appointment,' Janice lied.

The secretary's eyes narrowed. 'What time is your appointment?'

'Now.' Janice stabbed a look at a small wall clock above her. 'Two seventeen.'

The secretary raised an eyebrow. 'Two seventeen?'

Janice nodded. 'Two seventeen.'

'You must be mistaken, Gordon goes fly fishing on Thursday afternoons.' She smiled victoriously with all of her teeth. 'You can write Gordon a letter if you like.'

'Listen,' said Janice. She slammed her palm down on the secretary's tattered desk and a thin cloud of dust smashed into the air, and Blake wondered if the whole office might fall down. 'We're here to see Gordon, and we're not leaving until we do.'

'I'm afraid that's impossible,' the secretary said, still grinning gleefully. 'You can write Gordon a letter if you like.'

She looks like one of those carnivorous plants you'd find in a jungle, thought Blake about the secretary. *Harmless from a distance, but get too close, and snap...*

'Where's Blanche?' Janice asked, looking around. 'She knows me.'

'I'm sure I have no idea who you mean,' the secretary said.

'Small girl, blonde. Plays the viola.'

'You can write Gordon a letter if you like.'

Janice turned back towards Blake and Jan, throwing her hands up in silent frustration. *What now?* she mouthed at them.

'Let's go,' Blake said. He wanted out, he suddenly hated this place.

Janice's eyes flickered wet. 'But what about your note?' She looked like she might actually cry. Blake's heart twisted in his chest.

'We can come back another time,' Blake said. But of course, Blake knew the note would have an accident before then; burned or flushed down the toilet or sliced into pieces. He would take no chances; Janice would fish it out of the trash smeared with grease if she found it.

'You can write Gordon a letter if you like,' the secretary said again.

Janice span back to face her. For a second, Blake thought she might jab one of the secretary's eyes out with one of her long, pointing fingers.

'Gordon wrote *us* a letter, and we're sticking around until he comes back to tell us about it.'

It suddenly occurred to Blake the old woman would probably be able to read the note, that she would know Gordon's handwriting, but her face slammed shut like a book against Janice's aggression, much to Blake's relief.

'You're wasting your time,' she said. 'Gordon won't be back today.'

'There he is,' said Jan.

They all turned around. A middle-aged man with a mop of dirty grey hair stinking of the river had just walked in. He was in grey fishing gear, and busy with rods and nets with water trailing behind him, and he staggered into his office and shut the door, though it was mostly glass so they could still see him move around inside, like a spider in its aquarium.

'It looks like Gordon's in to me,' Janice said to the secretary, and then she folded her arms firmly across her chest as if to say, *I'm not going anywhere, you old crone.*

The secretary stood up, revealing her tiny stature, her head barely reaching Janice's elbow, a small grey blob against Janice's elegant length and big-eyed beauty. Now facing each other, their conflict seemed absurd; a slug against a praying mantis; no competition.

'I'll see what I can do,' the slug-woman said in a defeated voice. She walked over to the office and slipped through the door, and she and Gordon spoke with scattered looks in Blake's direction. The three of them, Blake, Janice and Jan, all reached for chairs and sat down, awaiting their fate.

'Last night I had Ruth Flinders,' Jan said in the silence when it stretched out too long.

'Oh yuck, why are you telling me *that*?' Janice cursed.

Jan scratched his head. 'Should I have said *made love*?'

'You shouldn't have said anything at all,' Janice said. 'You should have been a gentleman and kept quiet.'

The secretary emerged from the office. 'Gordon will see you in a few moments.'

Blake's blood became watery and his stomach churned. He stood and began to pace. Janice's annoyance radiated towards him, she hated it when he paced, it made her anxious, and her repressed hostility like heat only made Blake feel worse.

'Sit down, will you?' she snapped.

Blake felt his eyes drawn towards the door leading down into the street, and he thought of the cold sidewalk and the noise of the traffic, and how much he wanted to be in it, free and away from this place.

The Note

'What do you think's on your note?' Jan asked to fill the silence. Blake, still standing, could only manage a shrug. 'I guess you'll know soon enough,' Jan said guilelessly.

Yes you will. Because as it turned out, there was a man in New York who could tell you everything about yourself. He had an office in the corner of another office, he was guarded by a carnivorous plant-woman, he knew all the ways you hated yourself, and he was dressed in fishing gear that stunk of the river.

And here he is. Gordon leaned out of his office. 'You can come in now, young man.' It wasn't the voice Blake expected but high and sharp like broken glass. Blake wondered what that voice was about to tell him.

You really are a ghoul, aren't you?

Blake ran. He made for the door, pushed it open into the hot black corridor and went down towards the exit leading onto the street, the white glare of the outside shining through a frosted window. 'Where's he going?' Jan asked from behind, but Blake was already outside, his feet crunching down hard, brittle clumps of snow, staggering across the road through shrieking horns, hands shaking and lungs heaving, down an alleyway and out the other side. Catching his breath, he pulled the note from his pocket and stared at it.

Tear it up.

Two boys with hands bound in mittens and thick duffel coats saw him gasping against the wall. 'You alright, pal?' one of them asked.

'Sure, kid,' Blake said. And then, still crammed against the wall, he tore the note into a dozen stubby pieces, laughing all the way.

'Maybe he's loco,' one boy said to the other.

Blake let the note fall like powder into the snow, feeling free. The destruction hadn't been as satisfying as he had hoped; the crisp paper had turned to tissue through so much handling that in the end, it crumbled into dust.

Janice came jogging up the alleyway, a free hand against her hat. 'Scram, brats,' she said to the two boys. They shrugged at each other and walked off.

'Where's the note, man?' asked Jan, a few steps behind her.

Janice waved him into silence. She took a step towards Blake and stared at him with big wet eyes. 'Blake, honey,' she asked gently, 'what happened?'

Blake shrugged. 'It's just a fucking note, what do I care?'

Janice's face crumbled. Blake wasn't sure if she'd laugh or cry. 'You're such an odd little doofus,' she said eventually. She hugged him and kissed him on the cheek.

Jan stood scratching his head. 'I'm really confused right now.'

Janice laughed. 'You want some lunch, Blake?'

Blake thought he did. He thought about the Blue Box cafe with its towers of cakes on plates or Angelo's Deli, with its coils of German sausages and streaks of salty pastrami. 'Sure,' he said.

Janice looked around and saw that it was getting dark. The sun was sinking fast behind the cityscape and would soon plunge into the Hudson River. The day was nearly burned up; but for now, at least for the next hour, there was still time for something else.

ELIZABETH FREMANTLE

That Kind of Girl

'You look like that kind of girl,' is the first thing he says to me, shouting over the music and I just nod, wondering what he means or if I've heard right, not knowing how to talk to this man – because he *is* a man, with stubble and big hands – and he's looking at me, right at me, staring, making me feel nervous and he's, what, maybe twenty-eight, and he's got this bottle of, I don't know, vodka or something in his pocket, which he's swigging from and daring me, saying he bets I can't drink as much as he can, but 'I can,' I say, even though I don't know if I can, so I drink it to not look stupid, or young, when truth is I am both, and at some point he says, 'shall we go?' when I'm thinking we haven't even seen in the New Year yet but I must say yes, because he puts an arm round me, walking me across the sticky floor, barging past sweaty dancers, towards the exit where he is surprised when I say I don't have a coat and the cold blast of air in the street cuts right to the quick, so I'm glad to get inside his car, which has leather seats with a smell that makes me feel queasy, what with the vodka or whatever it was, and he drives very fast, so fast it scares me and when I say in a very small voice, 'Please can you slow down,' he goes faster, making me think he hasn't heard, so I shout, 'SLOW DOWN,' and he just laughs, going even faster and I'm nearly crying when we stop at his house, the whole house he lives in alone that has a carpet so thick my footsteps are silent as I follow him round, while he tells me about all the girls he's fucked in the different rooms and in different positions and one on the stairs who he fucked eight times in one night, or something, which he is very proud of and none of what he is saying is anything like what we learned about in PSHE, except the time Miss Knight tried to tell us about porn and went red and basically told us to avoid it or it would ruin our lives and started on about consent, as usual, and everyone was laughing about it together after class but not me because they don't really talk to me much, so while he's telling me about all the girls he's fucked and one woman, he says was forty – FORTY! – who's his neighbour and married with kids, I'm just trying to focus on staying upright, because I'm completely pissed, not to the point of throwing up but nearly, and have to concentrate very hard to get up the stairs where the bedroom is, which is where he starts to take my clothes off and I don't know why but I just let him do it, even though I don't really want him to and what I actually want is to go home but I don't dare tell him that because I'm already down to my knickers, and he asks me how old I am but when I tell him the truth he's shocked, smacks his forehead with the inside of his wrist and goes, 'fucking hell,' and turns to me asking, 'You a virgin?' so, after thinking about lying and deciding not to, I nod and he goes, 'fuck a fucking fuck,' and I say 'sorry,' and he goes, 'I'm knackered,' starting to get into bed, so not knowing what else to do, I get in too and stay as far as I can away from him, on the edge of the bed, which is against the wall on my side, worrying about what he'll do next but all he does is say, 'I won't do anything, just cuddle,' which makes me feel a bit better, and he goes on to pull me in, so his heavy arm is holding me tight and my head's on his chest, and he keeps on telling me stories about the fucks he's had and then one that particularly stayed in my head, which was about this girl who, 'Just sat down and had a piss,' while he was brushing his teeth, which he says was, 'disgusting,' and, 'A right turn off,' and he called a taxi and sent her home, and so we lie in silence with me thinking about that girl he sent home until he falls asleep but I can't sleep because of, well everything: the fact I'm in the bed of a strange snoring man, half stuck under his body, with a dead arm, afraid to move in case I wake him up and then what, so I lie still, dying for a pee more and more, until my fear of waking him is less than my fear of wetting the bed, forcing me to slide out from under him, careful, so careful not to disturb him, which I don't, and creep to the bathroom, where I run the tap, so he can't hear me pee in case he *has* woken up, before creeping back to lie awake until it's light and he wakes up, turning to me, eyes heavy, saying, 'Happy New Year,' and goes on a bit when we are in the car about not being able to believe it's next year already and I'm waiting for him to say something more, something nice, but all he says to me, as he drops me off near where I live, is, 'See you around,' but it isn't all bad because he takes his phone out, asking my number and says he'll text me so I have his, which he doesn't but he calls me two days later, wanting to take me out for a drive, only this time I say I won't come if he drives too fast and he says, 'Did I scare you?' but I don't want him to know he scared me, because if he knows how to scare me then what, and tell him: 'Don't be stupid,' and he drives quite slowly this time, telling me more stories, like about the time him and his friends drove around at night with a BB Gun, shooting at girls' bums – 'it was a right laugh', he snorts, and I am silent because what do you say when someone tells you that's what they do for fun, and he says, 'Don't say much do you?' when he drops me off and kisses me, a proper snog, making my stomach fizz, a feeling that keeps coming back, when I am in bed that night, wondering if he's my boyfriend, which he must be because he calls me again and takes me out again, and again and then he takes me to his friends' place where they all sit around listening to music and smoking weed and one of the girls asks me if I want some, so I take it, not to look like I don't know what I'm doing but it makes me cough my guts up and they all laugh making me want to be swallowed up by the armchair, but the same girl tells them to stop being mean and asks, 'How old are you, anyway?' and I tell her that I'll be sixteen in a week's time and they all laugh again but she calls them 'idiots' and when we are leaving I hear her asking my boyfriend what the fuck he thinks he's doing with me but he tells her it's none of her business and is clearly angry because he doesn't stop going on about it on the way to the car and drives fast again, so a big lump forms in my throat, not only because I'm scared but because he's taking me home, rather than to his place, where I haven't been back to since that first time, but I feel better when he drops me off and says, 'We'll do something special for your birthday, won't we, because you'll be sixteen,' which makes me smile as I get out of the car round the corner as usual, 'in case anyone sees us,' – which is pointless because nobody's ever at home – but I don't hear from him again for day after day and I feel as if my heart is breaking and I wish I'd had the guts to ask him for his number, because his number only ever comes up as: *No Caller ID*, but even if I had it I probably wouldn't have the guts to call it, and then, just as I'm losing hope, he *does* call saying, 'It's your birthday tomorrow and I promised, didn't I?' which makes me actually cry with happiness, but I do wonder if he is really going to come when he says he will, but he does, making my heart swell until I think it'll burst with love, and he takes me to his place again, where he gives me champagne, which I've never had before and I don't really like, and he says, 'I've never had a virgin, cos I've always thought a girl would get clingy but you're not like that,' before he turns me face down and fucks me, which hurts and my champagne spills all over my clothes, so they're still wet when he says he's got to take me home and I don't ask why I can't stay because I don't want to annoy him, but I tell him I'd rather get the tube, so he says, 'Suit yourself,' but it's freezing, so by the time I get home I'm so cold I can't get warm and the heating is off and no one's home, and I wait and wait for him to call me – I think I will wait forever – wondering if he's telling people about the virgin he fucked on her birthday, making me sadder and sadder and sadder and I know that I *am* that kind of girl.

RACHAEL FULTON

Call

The first call is OK. Hi Cathy it's Bill McManus here, I'm at The George. Hi pet. Aye sorry to bother you, Sarah needs picked up ah hink. She's a wee bitty upset, naw naw notae worry she's nae bother, nae bother at all, it's a hard time so it is. How've you been keepin? Oh aye, it's no easy, hi. Our Moira was the same for a long time aifter her mother. It's no the same but ken. Have you got the car? That's grand. Ahdtuckur masel but for the polis, Jim Wilson's git three points and that was the day aifter. That's grand see you shortly tahrah.

She curls in the passenger seat, face smashed in from crying and drink. Wine is the worst, it's always the worst, like pressing on bruises. Caaaathyyyy she sobs, tearing my syllables apart. Wet arms flail for me. Come on now. I plug her in. Come on, nearly home, don't cry, don't cry. No point crying.

That's a Dad phrase, no point crying. Autopilot response. I hear it before I know I'm speaking.

The next day she's at the foot of my bed. Skinny ghost, eyes near closed over. She looks 10 again after a nightmare.

I'm sorry Cathy, I really am, I'm so so sorry genuinely sorry I only went for the one and then I, then it was all – Shh, it's fine. Don't worry, I say, shh it's fine. Have you eaten anything.

Have you eaten anything. That's a Mum response and it's not even 8. We sit across from each other, stare into the muesli. The spoons do-si-do in the bowls clink clink. I've crushed one of Dad's tramadol into the milk to make her easier today, though I tell her I've none in the house.

Should I go away she says.

I look up from my bowl. All her drowning sultanas are rescued, lined up on the rim. Where would you go, I say, then realise No was the right thing.

In future I will wish I said yes. I take a mouthful of sultanas.

I don't know, she says. Anywhere.

There's only here though, for her. There is only this house with none of her things in it, all the dead people's stuff hidden away.

You think she's with Mum, Cathy? This time I know the thing to say.

Of course she is.

It's a lie, I don't believe it. Mum's buried in the plot on the hill, alone but for a clutch of wildflowers. Sarah's eyes are swimming, staring off at the kitchen chalkboard that shouts BINBAGS BLEACH DIET COKE. I want to make a crack that she's crying cause she wanted full fat, lighten the mood. I don't. I'm still learning OK things and not OK things. It's been 20 years. We knocked lumps out each other when she was last in this house. She gave me a black eye with a tennis racquet.

I run her a bath but make it shallow and leave the door open. Hard to tell how strong the cereal cocktail was or how hard it will hit her. I leave the radio on and make sure it's a talky one because she cries at all the songs, doesn't matter which ones. Even the happies remind her of car trips or musical statues or dressing up for school discos.

She burns all my good candles but tells me about the better ones she had in her old house and how she so adored them and maybe I should get one, the smell is so divine. I don't want a candle for eighty pounds. I don't want her divine familiar smells to fill the house and give her more reason to weep. I can smell the sea and the rain and the wind through the walls, it's why I didn't sell the house when Mum died. Sarah would prefer it too, if she lifted her head to notice. The city's ruined her. I tell her to go a walk down the beach, watch the waves for a time, see if it helps. She shakes her head.

The second call is still OK. Hello, Cathy? It's Paul, from The George. Yeah, sorry. Could you. That alright? Cheers. I go in and nod to everyone, Paul's got a cloth hand inside a pint glass and nods towards the toilets.
She's boo hoo hooing on the pan, door closed. Cartoon sad. Ahhh-haah-haaaaahhhh. It changes pitch. Sheila Sanderson's putting lipstick on at the mirror, hanging around like a bad yeast infection. She alright? She says through fillers with fake sympathy.

Aye, I say, though she's clearly not. All of Lochalsh knows she's not, or they will by the time Sheila's finished. I was sorry to hear about it, Sheila starts, but all I say is Mon out Sarah. Home time.

The door creaks. She's ashamed at her upset and ugliness. She cowers from Sheila Sanderson and the mirror. Sorry, sorry, sorry Cathy.

I nod at Paul on the way out, Thanks.

The next day she's got the cafetiere on, scrolling through her phone. Didn't want to wake you, she says, though the call woke me last night and this is just a different kind of waking. About last night, I'm sorry – Don't mention it, I say. It's fine. Do you want a muesli? I think about doubling her dose, save her whingeing and knock her clean out.

Have you spoken to the counsellor? I ask, though I know she hasn't. I'm just not up to it at the minute, she says, nursing the coffee. I take a slug of mine, it's tar.

Why don't you walk to the top of the hill then, I say. Look at the water, that's as good as therapy. Nature's therapy. And it's free. She says Not up to that either, and crumples her lip. I think, just up for drinking, not up for fixing. Just like Dad. I don't say it out loud.

She reads a book inside while I clean the gutters of rotting leaves. After an hour she's at the foot of the ladder and I nearly spook off it in fright.

It's normally just me and the cliffs here. The kites and buzzards are silent, the odd loud crow I chase off the fence in case it gets at the bins. Now she appears and evaporates everywhere like a sad shadow, humming or blaring something on speakerphone. Hey! she says which is the jump. Oh sorry, she says. I found this photo of Mum.

I don't look down, keep scraping the gutters. Yeah? Yeah.

I know she's been rooting around my drawers cause I hid everything the first night she came. Not just the expensive stuff. Anything would get her asking questions, spark her grietin again.

Nice photo of her, she says. It's got writing on the back. *Remember the shell.* What does it mean? Nothing, I say. Just put it back.

Don't believe you, she says.

Then it's just the scrape of dirt and moss from the gutters between us, debris of dead leaves cascading towards her. I don't look down. You can tell me, she says. I don't.

Third time. Hi there, it's Jill McMaster. Yes, sorry. She's not great. She was telling me bout whit happened, it's a damn sin. She's been a bit sick, bless her. No wonder she's upset. Is she on her own? No I know, of course. But the father? I see. God what a shame. How terribly sad. Lord.

She passes out in the passenger seat this time, slumps into the window with a glass clunk to the forehead. There's beige vomit in her hair. Don't piss yourself, I think, they're my jeans. I Fireman Sam her onto the couch. She's all bones these days, a tiny sparrow fallen limp on my shoulder. She wakes up in the recovery position, me holding her shoe.

CATHYYYY she says. I'm here I say. She's gooooone, she's goooonnne. I know, I say, I know. She's GOOONNE. I know. Come on, have some water. Come on. She takes a big gulp and lies back. She mutters some other slevered nonsense. I go to stroke her hair to make an effort, then remember the sick and withdraw my hand. I'm sorry, I'm sorry Cathy

She nestles into the cushions, soothed for a few minutes. Tell me about the photo of Mum she gulps through a sheet of snot. It goes quiet again. I don't want to tell her. Please, she says. How can't I know. Is it a secret? Get some sleep, I say. It's not fair, she says. None of it's fair.

In the morning she's out on the walkway overlooking the cliffs, grey layers of sea and sky stacked atop each other out into the distance. Gulls dive against the wind, rising and falling in the currents. She doesn't see them. She says sorry, sorry, I'm sorry it's like this Cathy. What am I gonnae do Cathy when will it stop? I don't say anything because I don't know. Spindly finger bones wrap round her head, Alkaseltzer fizzes in a glass.

I'm low on the other tablets, I should have rationed them. I wonder how long she will stay, when I can get the quiet back. She lights each new cigarette with the old, hand trembling, crumpling the fag dowts into the flagstones I paved for Mum's chair.

I should have brought her back here, she says, to meet you, to meet Mum. I shouldn't have stayed away so long, I just... Well you know what I was like and Lochalsh is hardly the place. I'm sorry for the way I left it. I should have come back for the funerals. You know how it is. I just couldn't be here anymore, you know?

I don't say anything. I've always been here.

Fifth time she doesn't make it to 9pm. There's folk in the restaurant still eating, says Paul, and...well. No disrespect here, ken. But. She's putting folk off their sticky toffee, talking about the wain. We've had a complaint. It's not her fault but, well, ken. I order a pudding for both of us, to take away, as a gesture, though she's stopped eating. She sees me walk into the pub and knows the game's up. I nod at Paul, though I'm sick of the sight of him. In the car she stares out the window and tells me all the lovely people she spoke to, how everyone was so so lovely, there was a really lovely woman called Jan. Same folk that complained about you ruining their pudding, I think, but I don't say it. She tells me Jan said Melissa sounded like a lovely wee lassie and we should have a local service for her, a memorial. Oh right, I say, but I hope she forgets, because it will be me that organises and it will only bring misery. You've still not told me about the photo of Mum, she says.

I got you a sticky toffee, I say.

In the days that follow she leaves the photo around the house for me to run into. More ghosts. Sometimes it faces out. On the beach smiling into the wind with a wild mane of hair, waving. Sometimes it's the words facing. Wobbly, almost indecipherable CATHY, REMEMBER THE SHELL Xx

Sarah's seething that I won't tell her about it, she has to force herself into everything, she won't let anything be. One afternoon I find the picture on my pillow. Piss off with the photo, I say. Tell me, she says. Why does it matter, I say. She was my mother too, she says. When it suited you, I think.

Seventh time, it's Geoff who owns the pub. This is getting a habit Cathy. I know, I say, as if it's my fault. As if she's a dog I've been letting shit in his garden. I ken she's been through a lot, he says. She has, I say. There's a long silence. See you shortly, he says. Click. She's outside when I get down there. The inside of her handbag's all over the pavement, her perfume's smashed glass everywhere. She cries as she stumbles into the car, pawing blindly for the handle. I'm sorry Cathy, she says. I'm sorry, I'm sorry. I'm soorryyyyy. Chinese water torture, that word. Nothing changes.

Eleventh. She's smoking in a huddle in the doorway when the car pulls up, staggering into the other folk, slevering shite. Loud spiky laughter in spurts like the caws of a crow. Come on, Sarah I say from the rolled down window. Get in the car. An old fella shouts TAXI'S HERE! thinks he's hilarious. They hook her arms and wobble her towards me, she near goes over on her ankle cause she wore a heeled boot. She says I'm not finished yet! I'm not ready to go home! Where's my fucking drink? They huckle her down to the passenger side. She's been crying but she's forgotten since, there are splats of mascara up her temples. Cathy why you here? You're such a fucking *spoil sport* Time to come home, come on I say. WHIT! I'm huvin a good time! I need to let my hair down sometimes you know! No-one else is having a good time, I say. Ah come on, you're my friends aren't you? She burls round to strangers as they smoke their fags to the letters. I'm not annoying you, am I? No, no, say the strangers but the faces say different. Get in the fucking car, I say. Eventually Paul's at the door saying We're not serving any more Sarah, you're sister's waiting for you, go on. Boooooooo she says, and falls backwards onto the ground with a clatter. The drunkards cheer WAYHEYYYY and everyone laughs at her. A force lunges in my chest, a dog straining to fight. I get out and drag her off the ground. THINK THAT'S FUNNY DO YOU I say to the clowns, and they shit themselves, even though I sound like my old maths teacher and I'm still wearing my slippers.

Fuck you, she says in the car and I know this is vodka talking now. I was having a good time. You're just jealous I've got friends. You've always been jealous of me. I swallow hard and steel my gaze onto the road ahead. Always deer and badger here and they make a right mess of the car. Aren't you going to say anything? she says. I don't say anything. Fine, fuck you. You never fucking say anything! You're such a BITCH. Do you even know what I've been through?! Melissa DIED. I don't say anything. I watched our parents die. I don't say anything.

In the morning she sleeps in. I fantasise about bludgeoning her with the old tennis racquet. There's no sorry or coffee waiting for me. I'm relieved for it. When she wakes she's in a black mood. Defiant. She thinks she has license to behave any way she likes. She's an adult, her child is dead. She should be able to have a drink when she wants to, she's a grown woman. Who the fuck am I to question her. She bangs things up and down on the surfaces, drags storms behind her.

I walk to the shore and stand into the wind, let Nature batter me as it has the cliffs for thousands of years. Salt and sand sting my skin, spray smashes against the still of the rocks, the almighty force of the ocean lands SMACK BOOM against the crags, withdraws, repeats, withdraws, repeats. When I get back she's sitting at the kitchen table, phone blaring a video about cats or some other nonsense.

I'll tell you about the shell, I say. Her head turns towards me, away from the video. She's thinner and thinner, I see the skeleton trying to burst through her skin. Another relative it falls to me to bury.

I'm listening, she says as if she has granted me her time, as if she is the Queen. I sigh. Remember we used to go walks on the beach with Mum, I say. Yes, she says, to see the dolphins. For the sea, I correct her, we went because Mum loved the sea.

We never saw any dolphins, she says, huffing.

Nothing has changed in 30 years. The world exists to please her.

It was never about dolphins, I say. It was the sea. Mum just told you we would see dolphins so you'd leave the house. The water here's no use for them. She made the dolphins up.

Oh. Sarah looks confused. Affronted.

Anyway, I say, after you left. We did the walk just the two of us. Then every day after Dad died. We'd walk along and watch the waves. And– Telling her is a bad idea, but I'm too far into it.

And? And. When she was, when she. When she started getting unwell, when she couldn't walk anymore, we couldn't go together, so I'd just go myself, but I'd bring a wee shell back for her. We'd kid on they were phones. I know it's daft. She said I could pick up a shell and talk through it, tell her how wild the wind was or what the sky was doing, if I'd found a starfish or funny lump of driftwood or a bit sea glass or something. Just silly things. She said I would hear her talk back. When she was getting worse she said...Well. She said when she was gone, when she was dead I mean, it would still work. That when I wanted to tell her how the sea was doing I could just pick up a shell and she'd be at the other end.

It is quiet but for the wind. My eyes flit up towards my sister. She is still.

And that's the last thing she ever wrote down, and it's the last thing she ever said out loud. So. That's that. That's why I keep it, I say.

Then I'm finished and it's quiet. Sarah looks unnerved by my confession. The wind howls around the house, rattling windows, creaking timber. Did it work? She says. What? I say. The shell. Did you hear her. It's made up Sarah, I say. It's not real.

Outside the sky is slate. The wind is thundering the walls, full of hard water now which it hurls against the glass. Sarah sits staring out with the photo in her hand, tapping it on the side of her leg, reading it, turning it, reading it again, reading it, turning it, tapping.

Do you think this was how it was always going to end up? she says. I don't say anything, I don't know the right thing to say.

She puts on a jacket. I'm going out, she says.

Drinking? I say.

Mind your own business, she says, though it always ends up my business.

There is no twelfth call.

SARAH HARTE

The Graduation

She doesn't know yet that he has died. In a tony suburb facing the Dublin hills it's a graduation party. The Villa is crammed with young people milling in joyful configurations. More file in carrying plastic bags and back packs. Stationed next to the window, Oonagh sees them arrive, passing the monkey puzzle tree. Her brother in law talks about his son's future career in The City. She was ambushed by him. She listens, querulously passive, to the back and forth between him and another man. 'He did a master's in finance at Smurfit. He got a First,' her brother in law says, his eyes resting briefly on her. These rehearsed lines will be repeated many times. The unspoken theme is that the young man is a winner. Her brother in law who is a banker regards poverty as a moral failure. Like him, her nephew will dedicate himself to the art of making money. The other man, Adrian talks about his offspring, it's the usual schtick of law, medicine, and business. She ransacks their sentences for something to say, scanning the room preparing herself for imminent departure. But Adrian smoothing his hair back says. 'What's your boy up to now Oonagh?'

'He's mediocre like us,' she says, although she considers her son to be unique. 'The apple doesn't fall far from the tree.' This momentarily silences them.

'I wouldn't say that,' her brother in law says. 'That seems a bit harsh.' Although fiscally a success, her brother in law is incapable of thinking through the simplest thing, irony is lost on him. She leaves them to their unreflecting pleasure in success and in themselves. As always, she wonders how her sister married him. She thinks that in her position she might affix masking tape to his mouth, but he would probably continue to opine. Oonagh's daughter swoons past wearing few clothes, a spiky mass of hair and insolence. Her skin is the colour of a satsuma although specks of white on her ankles give them a pebble-dashed look. 'Piss off Mum. You haven't a clue,' she said earlier when Oonagh suggested a less heavy hand with the tan. At fifteen, her primary preoccupation is the male gaze. The young men drink beer, indifferent to her allure. Oonagh does a circuit of the party, enjoying brief chats. She's fixing herself a vodka with soda and fresh lime when her phone pings. The text is from an old friend; Frankie has killed himself. She reads the text processing the words before

The Graduation

stepping outside. Late August. Humid with a strong wind. The trees are rustling. A briny tang in the air, the sea is nearby. Nightfall. Both students in UCC long ago, Oonagh and Frankie had an on off thing for years. Afterwards she read about him. That he made serious money. That things went wrong. Maybe there's a domino effect, one thread unravels, then another, she doesn't know. Several blurry moments elapse before she calls the man who sent the text. 'It's on the radio. The police had to kick the door down.' Blood crashes in her ears she closes her eyes. 'It's awful isn't it?' he says. 'Can you believe it? Of all people.' Burgers sizzle on a grill, releasing their meaty aroma, a spatula held by somebody's arm flips them. Voices seem faraway, sounds intermingle. Her surroundings come lose. She listens to the voice on the other end of the phone, he mouths platitudes. Last Christmas, she bumped into Frankie on Grafton Street. He was buying a present for his daughter. 'Would you have a look at this dress Oonagh?' he said. 'Give me a second opinion. She's a demon to buy for.' She followed him into the shop noticing his unshaven face, how his weight had ballooned, thinking it odd he should solicit her advice. 'I'm hopeless at these things.' The tang of beer. She steered him towards a more suitable choice. The present was parcelled up. He suggested a drink. 'Two old pals having a Christmas drink.' They ducked into the snug at the back of Kehoes, dark wood, the faint smell of Guinness farts, old memories, the pub a Victorian shrine. The wife had left. 'A bank sent in the receiver,' he said turning around from where he stood at the hatch ordering drinks. 'They changed the locks on the office building without even telling me. I nearly had a heart attack. If they'd even picked up the phone and let me know.' Oonagh has noticed how identification with a set of economic expediencies increases capacity for rationalisation of indefensible practices. It's a topic her brother in law could give a dissertation on she thinks, her eyes moist. 'Keep in touch,' the man she called says. 'I'll see you at the funeral.' She hangs up, there's nothing more to say. Oonagh holds her phone in dazed confusion before walking to the end of the garden towards inky shapes, towards the smell of pot. 'May I?' she asks, so the young men clustered behind a clump of trees look unsure. A young man with a sensitive look hands her a joint. She exhales, trying to picture Frankie's face. He was good looking back in the day with dark eyes, and a muscular build, he was smart too. They had more than one drink in the snug, he kept ordering rounds. She went home half-cut, leaving a bag of presents behind. 'This dope is too strong for me,' she says handing it back. 'Thank you.' She pauses. 'Life is short, don't turn into assholes.' She feels eyes on her retreating back. Frankie had his public self-stripped away. She never checked on him. She doesn't want to elevate the significance of her connection to Frankie, to adopt the mantle of chief mourner but she asks herself why she didn't call. 'We should do this again Leggy Oonagh,' he said on taking leave of her. He seemed delighted to have met her. 'It's a date,' she said. 'Be there or be square.' Some blarney like that, although she planned to follow up on it. She remembers him turning on the street, as she did to wave.

Back inside the house she fixes herself a large vodka, gulping it down, then has another. She finds her husband who is exiting a bathroom, telling him the news. She feels in danger of being derailed. 'I'm sorry,' he says. Once when she was very pissed, she said that she thought Frankie might be the one that got away. She apologised afterwards. She doesn't like to see the pity spreading behind her husband's eyes, Frankie wasn't somebody to be pitied. Anything but that. 'I don't want to talk about it,' she says.

She finds her sister but finds herself unable to voice the news, although Frankie was her friend too. She listens to her sister and some rail-thin woman discuss marathon running. Running, Oonagh has observed is taken up in the middle years by successful people who don't read; there's a whiff of the mid-life crisis about it. She stares at a new painting on the wall as they discuss their personal bests. The house is full of the accretions of a long marriage and her sister's shopping habit. Oonagh feels in some bottomless space. When a gap opens, she says. 'Next you will do The Camino'. Her sister's eyebrows lift. This is not what she meant to say, she doesn't want to swamp their conversation. Her face is stiff with strain. Her brother in law materializes in front of them. His expression is solemn, but it's obvious that he's enervated. Oonagh decides he knows about Frankie. When he speaks, he has the muted excitement of somebody passing on bad news. 'Frankie Barron has been found dead in his flat.' Her sister's hand is covering her mouth. He checks Oonagh's reaction. 'You used to knock about with him, didn't you?' Oonagh draws in her breath deeply.

'The developer,' her sister's friend says.

Her brother in law nods. 'Looks like he killed himself.'

'Oh Oonagh, that's shocking,' her sister says her mouth forming an O. 'Frankie, is the last person....' She trails off. Oonagh wonders if Frankie banked with her brother in law. She knows this is simplistic, he probably banked with many financial institutions and yet. Oonagh's hand grasps her other wrist. She imagines people picking over his carcass, saying things like 'suicide is so selfish.' She has never understood this point of view, is that final act not borne out of complete desperation? She imagines sirens roaring down the road, she resists imagining a reconstruction. 'You never know what's under the bonnet,' her brother in law says shaking his

The Graduation

head. *Now* he's a psychologist, he has always overestimated his skill in all things, she thinks how Frankie was the opposite. Despite the moving and shaking, there was always a chink in Frankie's armour, this was what she found attractive.

'Makes you want to run an inventory over your life,' Oonagh says fixing eyes with her brother in law. She feels her throat closing. 'Come here to me,' her sister says putting an arm around her but Oonagh wrests away. She makes her way to the living room where a smattering of young folk dance. The carpet has been rolled up, the furniture pushed back or taken from the room. A lone disco light flashes from the corner. Others dot the periphery. She takes off her shoes and throws them, missiles rocketing through the air. One shoe hits a Patrick Scott painting, tilting its gold disc to the side. This provokes a rustle of self-conscious laughter. 'Are you okay Auntie Oonagh?' her nephew asks.

'I'm above ground,' she says giving him the thumbs up. She remembers that she and Frankie fought a lot. 'You're addicted to drama,' he said once. He accused her of being too intense. She sees her daughter sprawled on a velvet sofa, then sitting up, looking appalled at this maternal lack of dignity. Oonagh waves at her daughter who glowers back. A magnificent looking young woman, in dungarees hair streaming down her back dances with abandon. Oonagh follows her lead. Her daughter tugs at her sleeve. 'You're drunk Mum,' she says. 'I'm getting Dad.'

'I'm okay Pet.' Some minutes later her husband is at her elbow come to hustle her home. 'You got a good one there,' her aunt said once.

'You're teaching tomorrow Missus,' he says. He gives a half smile. 'I'm under orders.'

'I'll cope,' she says. 'Take the Gestapo home. She has school tomorrow.' Oonagh dances away from him. She wants a night off from being a mother, a wife. She's looking back, remembering him and all that went before. She thrusts her arm up in the air. She instructs her nephew to play *Your song*. 'The Billy Paul version.' When it finishes, she says. 'Play it again.'

She dances, mad disconnected thoughts rocketing through her mind. She wonders what all the striving is about, when everyone is on a collision course with death? Her sister comes into the room, she imagines to smooth things over; her sister has always been the peace maker in the family. But her sister is telling her son to 'crank up the volume.' And she takes Oonagh's hand, squeezing it. 'Frankie loved to dance,' Oonagh says. Her sister nods, her face clenched in sadness. The sisters dance until the underside of their hair is wet. From the corner, she sees her brother in law's face until it's a smudge. She pictures a young Frankie dancing dipped in light, at twenty-two or three, with a shorn head, the shifting uncertainties in his face that she loved momentarily banished, his dark eyes gleaming in Sir Henry's, a club they loved, the centre of their universe, now gone too. Beside them in the drawing room, the dazzling overgrown children with cloudless young faces dance immune to the dangers and sorrows the world dishes out, believing that life goes on and on.

NIDA MANZOOR

Sandals

He is wearing sandals. His hairy toes pinned down by leather straps. I am in finery. Itchy finery that Mama has picked out; a salwar-kamiz that has a built-in bra that rounds my tits off in a parabola that I think looks unnatural. Could I marry this man? His hair is gelled flat save a few prongs at the front that are erect. My hair is long again, curly, thick and annoying. It is heavy around my shoulders. Mama thought I should straighten it, but then decided it probably best for him to see my natural hair. His arms are skinny and jutting out at the elbows. My arms are thin and tapering though I believe them to be fat. I could totally marry him. Why not? Aunties had winked at me when news of our meeting had disseminated. *He's very well to do*, they said. Well to do. It's aunties like these saying shit like 'well to do' that is responsible for the incessant Jane Austen and Shakespeare adaptations set in modern day South Asian communities. Maybe all it takes is for one rogue auntie to wink at me and say something like 'he looks like he'll shag your brains out' to put an end to it once and for all. In truth, I don't think this man is capable of shagging my brains out. I mean – he's wearing sandals. It's the kind of footwear that betrays a severe lack of game. I'm one to talk – I'm here like a festooned doll, bound and glittering like a trophy bell-end and he's wearing fucking sandals. He's also wearing a hoodie but it's those sandals that are hollowing out my insides.

He's been smiling at me as though I were a cute puppy ever since I sat down which I find deeply disconcerting. Would I prefer he was smiling at me more creepily, like I was a lunchable? Nope. Would I prefer he wasn't smiling at all, like some serious religious fundamentalist incapable of levity? Certainly not. Maybe puppy-smiling is the only modus operandi to be had, but why am I so unsettled? I don't know – maybe it's because he's American. Smiley motherfuckers who secretly want to hoard gold and cackle into characterless Suburban houses. That's rich coming from me – a Brit. The world's great pestilence, the Brits. Pissing all over the planet like an overzealous terrier. No Baba, I don't think it's astounding that they gave us bridges and roads. Fuck bridges and roads.

Sandals may be American, and I may be British, but it should be noted that our ancestors are from the same shitty, little Indian-turned-Pakistani village so we're probably related and destined to have deformed offspring.

Apparently Sandals made some serious coin via Silicon Valley geekery, which is why he has been bestowed with the title of 'well to do'. I am indifferent to wealth when it comes to the men I go for, which Baba thinks is a serious shortcoming. He blames himself, saying that he spoiled me. Because I've never felt the wolf at the door I don't appreciate the true importance of wealth in a prospective spouse. I don't think I buy this argument. In my mind it's Mama's fault I'm not that into stuff, because she was never really into stuff. Every time Baba returned home from his travels abroad, he furnished Mama with trinkets and bags and other expensive bollocks. Although Mama received said bollocks with Austenian good grace, her smiles were pure fakery. I could tell. I have always been surprised that Baba could never tell. I should point out, although I don't care for wealth, I am attracted to the idea of being a gold-digger. There's callousness in the role of gold-digger that I find admirable. A no-bullshit contract between gold-digger and gold-diggee – I want your money, you want my youth/beauty/charm/wit/pussy. Transparency. The pinnacle of honesty. I respect that.

I don't think I am physically attracted to Sandals, but I suppose that doesn't matter. What is attraction anyway? Hormones, chemicals, enzymes – bullshit really. Physical attraction fades eventually so why not save the disappointment? I'm sure there's a charming spot on the ceiling I could stare at if we were ever engaged in intercourse. I'm sorry. I don't mean to be so, what's the word, nihilistic? Glib? Is it boring? It's probably really fucking boring.

Ok so yeah I had a breakdown, which is why I'm here. Final year of med school and I had a breakdown. Pretty standard stuff, not all that uncommon really. You know that feeling when anxiety becomes deafening, like the sound of crickets in the night and fuck me, it feels like you're in a rickety tin-can cockpit jettisoned off a spaceship hurtling towards the earth, moments away from exploding into fragments of fiery detritus? Yeah, you know. Having a breakdown was the only option I had.

So here I am, staring at the toes of the man I might marry. Don't get too excited, you wankers, it's not a forced marriage; keep it in your pants. This isn't Heathcliff on the Moors. This is just some hairy toes and a glittery fool. Maybe I'll bear him a bunch of kids and then peace out, leaving him in his San Francisco bungalow to raise the very brood I birthed out of my vagina whilst I join the Scientologists and give those aunties something meaty to gossip about. Maybe I'll marry him and we'll share the workload and childcare and be a great fucking partnership, equals or whatever, and when I'm old and on my deathbed and staring into the eyes of my grown-up children, I'll blow my brains out because I'll realize it wasn't worth a goddamn thing.

Sandals is trying to impress Mama by telling her about the humanitarian branch of his tech company. She is smiling with calm interest, nodding and saying hmmm/wow/how interesting. Mama doesn't give a shit about humanity, you dumb bitch, she only wants to trick you into marrying her broken daughter. Moi. I take a moment to appreciate how impressive Mama is. She has managed to spin my mental breakdown and subsequent dropping out of uni into social acceptability by telling everyone "she wants to settle down and start a family, so has decided to pause her studying for the moment". God. That was some serious PR heavy lifting. If anything it feels like my cachet has gone up. The only thing better than a medical student is a young woman ready for insemination. The truth is, I do not want to be a mother. I just don't find it very natural. It's creepy. You have a literal parasite in you, feeding off your life force. Akin to a tape worm. How is that ok?

You're probably thinking, why then are you entertaining this marriage nonsense? Why then are you misleading these innocent parent figures and hairy-toed technotwats into thinking you'll be a blushing bride and mother of children? Why? Why fucking not, I say. Aren't you curious to know what would happen if you kept saying yes and yes and yes? Following the path of least resistance, allowing yourself to tumble through time and space, seeing how many hits you can bear as you fall. Once, when I was thirteen, when we were on a family holiday in the Canary Islands, I swam out to sea. I just kept swimming away from the shore. I could see the water get darker, I could feel the water get colder as I got deeper. I could feel my heart rate pound as fear pulsed through me. But I kept going, further and further into the blackness, desperate to know how far I could I go. Even when the water started to toss me about and pull me down, I kept going, you know? Just me and my life in some epic game of chicken. It's sort of like that, I guess. When do you bail? Who wins? How far is too far? I need to know. I always need to know.

LAURANE MARCHIVE

Milk

7:15 am. The co-working open space is still empty, great green plants hanging from mezzanines and long large tables of white wood. Mikha swings by the locker room to drop his coat. He forces his bag into the narrow silver locker. As he takes off his scarf, a sharp pain slides across his abdomen, so bright he has to place one hand on the wall to steady himself. He sits down. Just for a second, just to catch his breath. He unzips his hoodie, lifts his t-shirt. When he pokes the flesh around his belly button, he can almost see it: a white shape, travelling under the skin. Mikha looks up, counts to ten. On the ceiling, a lightbulb is missing. When he looks down again, the white shape is gone. The skin is clear and smooth, not even a ripple.

He comes out of the locker room, makes his way to the coffee stand. The machines shine in hammered chrome, the overhead sign reads 'Coffeed-Up!' John is already there, leaning on a bench, playing on his phone.

'Morning!' John chirps.

'Morning.' Mikha ties the branded apron around his waist. He moves slowly, his eyes burning. John starts telling him about a movie he watched last night. About a new girl he's been texting. About an article he read, that says water can feel things but London water is so polluted it's basically mud, basically depressed. Mikha only half listens. On the counter, he arranges the jars of tea bags, napkins, wooden spoons and coco flakes. When he lifts a small bag of sugar to refill one of the jars, the bag bursts. Sugar spills everywhere.

John gives him a sideways glance.

'Dude, you look like shit.'

'I know, I'm just tired,' Mikha says, pushing sugar into the bin.

1 pm. Across the open space, strangers in small groups discuss unrelated things. They talk about their work or their next project. They sport fancy smart coats and designer hoodies. They ask for long blacks or lattes, cold press, green tea, sugar, no sugar, an avalanche of cardboard sleeves. Mikha pours cup after cup after cup, eyes on the froth that forms at the surface. Every so often, the smell of hot milk; a churning deep in his

stomach. The room is so big and so wide it should echo but doesn't: the walls are clad in sound-dampening tiles that swallow up noise and spit it back out as a nice homogenous buzz.

When the post-lunch rush dies down, Mikha bites into a cream salmon bagel. His phone vibrates on the counter.

Katie:
How is it going?

Mikha moves away from John. Wipes his hands clean on his apron.

Good!
At work. You?

Good :)
So, I have a surprise…

Ha
What's that?

Guess…

:) ?…

I am coming to London this weekend!!!

Mikha stares at the phone. Katie doesn't usually use multiple exclamation marks. She's a stickler for punctuation, multiple exclamation marks simply aren't correct. John's elbow gently pokes into his rib.

'Everything ok?'

'What?' Mikha startles, he puts the phone away. 'Yeah it's just… it's my mum,' he lies. 'It's nothing.'

John looks at Mikha's face.

'All good, man,' he laughs. 'You just looked a bit freaked out, that's all.'

11 pm. Turning the water off. Leaning back to catch the towel. Dark blue. Stripes. Relatively new so it's still soft and plush, welcoming and comfortable but not particularly good at catching droplets. Mikha runs the fabric along his legs, the small of his back, the soft of his armpit. In the mirror, the stubble on his face looks patchy. He took up climbing a few months back, but his silhouette is still soft, the arms long and thin, the upper body smooth and undefined. Pinching the skin at the waist, the fingers leave a red mark. He turns off the bathroom light. Bedroom. Sits down on the bed.

Katie:
Are you dead :) ?

                                Sorry, just been busy all day

Ah ok

...

 Are you in London this weekend?
It would be nice to see you.

Mikha lies down, holds his phone above his face. His stomach twists but he smiles, sparkles of adrenaline buzzing at his ears. Still, he waits, fingers hovering above his screen, before replying:

                        Definitely!
                        What's the occasion?

It's my brother's birthday.
I told him I'd come down

                        Sounds good

Does it?
You don't seem too excited

                        I'm excited!
                        ...
                        … a bit nervous

Nervous is good, I guess?

Katie sends a selfie, smiling, feigning surprise, a rounded mouth, pouting. Her face is little and symmetrical. Like a soft pretty mouse. Her hair dark, curly and shiny in the light. Her skin pale and cream-like. She looks sweet, she always looks sweet, she *is* sweet, and quick-witted and sharp but also shy. On the picture, she wears silky grey pyjamas.

                    You look nice :)

Mikha zooms in on the shot, tries to picture it as a moving image. He first saw Katie at a party, but back then, they didn't talk. Mikha doesn't do too well at parties, or in crowds or in groups; whenever a room gets too busy, he shuts down, the noise bleeds into his ears and everything becomes blurred. So he listens and he laughs and he nods, but mostly he just drinks and floats to the sound of whatever is playing. At some point that night, John walked past and said, 'Have you seen Katie?' and Mikha asked, 'Who's Katie?' John said, 'My sister. Green top, curly hair?' Mikha replied, 'I didn't know you had a sister.'

Milk

Then he saw her. She was drinking red wine, her mouth stained at the corner. He spent an hour watching her move through the living room: she would stand at the edge of every conversation, always in the vicinity but rarely jumping in, her fingers curled against the stem of her glass. After a few beers, he went home and forgot about her. But a few days later, she popped up on his feed: a picture from the weekend, pretty. Standing next to John, drunk. In the picture, she was laughing. She looked friendly, approachable. It made him want to know her.

           Do you think water has feelings?

What?

           Water. Someone told me it can feel stuff.
           Feel depressed and stuff.
           You think?

Err...
I don't think so.

           Yeah, me neither.
           I was just wondering.

At the party, he overheard a conversation. She was complaining about the online dating scene in Edinburgh, it was so small you kept bumping into the same people, honestly, a nightmare. The following week, he created a dating account. His phone automatically loaded pictures onto his profile: the first image black and white, his face partially hidden. The second one, backpacking in Europe. The third one taken by John, sitting in front of a half-finished slice of pizza. Mikha scrolled through his photos. All the pictures showed someone quiet, someone who looked younger than his age. Someone with only a handful of friends and no unique features. Someone who just wasn't interesting.

What about plants. Do you reckon
they can feel stuff?

           No, plants are definitely stupid.
           Obviously.

What?
What are you even talking about
Plants are great.

Mikha closes the chat window, opens Instagram. He pushes a finger into his abdomen to quiet down the churning. Opens the man's account.

Mikha doesn't personally know the man. One day, he was scrolling through Instagram, and he stumbled upon his profile. The man is a documentary maker based in Paris and London, who often travels around the world on various projects. The man likes long walks in the countryside and has a nut allergy. The man is attractive, nothing out of the ordinary but he looks good in pictures. The man is interesting without being arrogant. Successful without being famous. Confident without being annoying. Good looking without being full of himself. Most importantly, Mikha and the man have no friends or contacts in common.

The light in the bedroom is so bright and yellow Mikha has to shield his screen with his hand. He scrolls down the man's Instagram. Looks for the right picture, finds it: a walk, smiling in front of winter London trees. Their silver branches covered in frost. He takes a screen shot. Reframes the image. Makes it imperfect, and sends it to Katie.

> Went for a walk today
> Check out those trees!

Wow so pretty
Is it snowing in London? It's raining here.

Mikha looks out the window. It's only raining, but it doesn't matter. Katie won't check. She never does.

After creating the dating account all those weeks ago, Mikha had replaced all the pictures on his new profile with a picture of the man with a dog. A picture of the man next to a large video camera. A picture of the man trekking in a forest, carrying a large rugged backpack complete with rolled-up sleeping mat and dangling metal cup. In the description, he wrote 'Traveller at heart. Still fairly new here...love meeting new people.' He set his location to Edinburgh, his range to 5 miles.

He swiped for three days straight. On the fourth, he found Katie.

2 am. Outside Mikha's window, the howling is back. A sharp, grey sound, heavy like a scrape. People in the neighbourhood call it 'The Cow from Hell'. It always comes at night so you can't really see it, but you can hear it: a great big wounded animal, calling and screeching. As it turns out, it's just the sound of TFL cleaning the nearby train tracks; they send round this giant mechanical beast that slowly crawls up and down the rails, scraping off the dust, the dirt. Mikha hears it often. But he also knows that TFL can't be cleaning the tracks that relentlessly.

He tries falling back asleep but his eyes won't stay closed. Sometimes, in the middle of the night, he finds himself glancing at his phone, in case Katie can't sleep either. In the evenings, she often sends him pictures of herself in her Edinburgh flat. Or pictures of herself with her pet bunny. Or pictures of her bedside lamp when it glows in the night, and the room is dark and the light casts on the wall a shape that looks like a tree.

In exchange, Mikha makes up stories for her, weaving colourful tapestries for her to get lost in. He invents the travels the man goes on: Paris for the weekend, he sends her a picture of the great black rats that run around Notre-Dame at night. A few days in Lisbon; he sends a selfie of the man smiling on the beach. Mikha has become good at travel blogs, at backpacker hashtags. For Katie, he curates an exciting entity that feels closer to him than the real Mikha. But there are also some truths, things he can't tell anyone else. Like how his only family is his one sister, but she has a husband and a baby and lives on the other side of the world, so they don't talk that often. How he hates small dogs because they always look scared. And how sometimes at night, he can't sleep for hours and hears weird sounds that probably aren't there.

3:34 am. Mikha sits up. Kitchen. His belly aching, he strokes the skin. Inside, something makes its way along the cavities. He pours himself a glass of water. The smell of rice and leftover grease logged in the drain is sweet, rotten. Underneath his t-shirt, the shape is visible now. It ripples, pinches at the lining of his stomach. Mikha braces himself against the edge of the sink and opens his mouth. He bends over the metal hole, all the muscles cramping, cramping, heaving, but nothing comes up.

A slow sliding. Whenever Mikha takes off his clothes at night, the lump pokes through the skin, gliding on the wrong side.

'What the fuck are you?'

Mikha pushes down on the white shape and it disappears again. He opens the cutlery drawer. Takes out a fork. When the shape reappears near his belly button, he pokes it; the shape recoils. A few weeks back, when the shape first appeared, Mikha did some research. Online, someone said you can get terrible parasite worms from eating bad meat, and the only way to get rid of them is to wait in front of a bowl of warm milk, mouth open. When it smells the milk, the worm travels up the throat and the moment it pokes out its head, you just close your jaws and snap its head off.

Mikha tried it for three nights in a row and nothing has come yet. But what else can he do. He pours the milk in the pan. Opens his mouth, wide, as wide as he can. He can feel the shape, wanting and curling, travelling through his intestines, smelling the milk and crawling upwards. But whenever it nears the edge, Mikha can't stand it. His body refuses, and he just coughs and retches.

6:45 am. When he walks into Manor House station, the speakers blast ominous classical notes. Mikha presses himself against other bodies, his skin burning in the heat of the carriage. At Holborn, people wait in line or in crowds for a chance to get on the escalator. Stepping out onto the street, a frozen windy slap; the crowd pours out onto the pavement like liquid.

Next to John, Mikha pours espresso after espresso. The queue so busy all they do is press and pour for one, two, three hours. Every time Mikha has to froth milk, the shape turns and curls inside him.

'You're coming to the party tonight?' John asks when the rush finally slows down.

'What party?'

'Dude,' John frowns. 'My birthday?'

Mikha apologises, 'Of course man,' he says. 'I'll be there for sure.'

In his pocket, his phone buzzes.

Katie:
Hello!
So about this weekend
Tell me when/where you wanna meet?

Mikha puts the phone on the counter, face down. Around the coffee stand, people eat their packed lunches on wide benches. They act like they own the space, the light, the very ground they walk on. A few metres away, a pretty blond woman is talking to someone. She rearranges a strand of loose hair, neatly folding it behind her ear.

'Do you know her?' John asks.

'Who?'

'That girl you're looking at.'

'What?' Mikha says. 'I wasn't looking...'

The pretty blond woman waves in their direction. John waves back.

'She's really nice,' John says when she disappears towards the elevators. 'Black Americano, no sugar.' He looks at Mikha. 'She's coming tonight,' he adds. 'You should talk to her.'

Mikha bites into one nail; it gives in under the pressure of his teeth. He opens his mouth to say something, but inside his body, the shape moves. It pushes against his stomach, trying to get out. Mikha braces himself against the counter. He clenches his mouth shut. His throat makes noises he doesn't recognise. Choking noises. John grabs his shoulder, starts shaking him.

'Mikha! Fuck man, are you ok?'

He can feel that John is trying to wrap his arms around him. That John is inches away from improvising a Heimlich manoeuvre.

The shape recoils.

Recoils and hides, deep inside his stomach.

'I'm ok,' Mikha breathes, pushing John away, 'I'm fine.' He wipes the saliva beaded across his lips.

John's face is red, worried. He offers Mikha a tissue.

'Are you sure you're fine?' John asks. 'You've been really quiet recently,' he whispers, 'and you've stopped staying for drinks after work... is something going on? Because if something's going on, I wish you'd just–'

'Honestly,' Mikha says, 'leave it.' He takes the tissue and smiles. 'Everything is fine. Ok?'

Ok?

Katie:
Hey

                        How is it going

Yeah good. You?

                        Yeah, really good. Tired though
                        Long day at work :/

Oh, sucks.
...
So tomorrow?

                        Yes

I'm so excited!
Still want to meet up?
We could go get a drink somewhere?

Hello?

Hey, is everything ok?

Helloooo?

10:30 pm. When he gets to John's house for the party, Mikha rings the doorbell and a woman he doesn't know opens the door. She wears giraffe earrings and lets him in without interrupting her conversation with a man whose bottle of beer is almost empty.

The living room is full of people holding mismatched cups. John stands next to the window, vaping, chatting to the pretty blond woman from the co-working space. Mikha walks into the kitchen, puts down a plastic bag full of beer. Around him, the conversations are opaque. In the ground floor bedroom, the bed is covered in coats, and on the first floor, all the bedrooms are locked. He climbs to the second floor. On the left-hand side, the sound of conversations floats from a door left ajar; a shard of orange light encroaches on grey carpet. Mikha pushes the door; inside, a few people are sitting on the bed, on the floor or at the desk. He hears the words 'tornado', 'climate change' and 'sharks.' As he steps into the room, all the faces turn to him and he counts six pairs of eyes. Nearest to the window, one of the pairs is Katie's. She looks at him, briefly, before turning back towards the man sitting near the desk.

Mikha asks:

'Can I join you?'

But nobody hears. Then a girl looks up and shuffles to the right so he can sit next to her.

'Sharks aren't endangered, are they?' A woman in a woollen jumper asks.

The man sitting next to the desk swivels on his chair.

'I didn't say they were endangered, but with the temperature of the oceans rising, you'd definitely expect their population to drop, wouldn't you?'

The room nods in agreement. From where he is, Mikha can see the details of Katie's body: the soft wrinkles at the knuckles of the fingers, the thin hair rising from her forearms, the creases of her skin at the neck. The light coming from the desk lamp changes colour every few seconds, now orange now blue now purple, casting strange shadows on her face, painting her hair red or green or grey. She looks different from the pictures. Less perfect, more rounded, less angular. When the light turns red, she looks towards Mikha and he barely recognises her. But then the light softens into orange and she looks so much like the last picture she sent him that his throat contracts.

Underneath his shirt, the shape curls.

'Octopuses are smart, though,' she says, and when she speaks, her voice is unfamiliar. A little louder than he remembered. 'They can open jars with their tentacles. People shouldn't eat them, really.'

She brushes something from the sleeve of her jumper. Someone replies that octopuses are smart but so are pigs, plus calamari rings are tasty so really, what can you do, and Mikha tries to think of something to say and that calamari is squid, not octopus, but his voice sticks on his tongue.

11:30 pm. Katie says she needs some air, and Mikha says, 'yeah, me too.' He follows her down the stairs. He doesn't have a plan, not exactly, but if they could just talk in private, he knows he might be able to make her laugh. To make her interested in him, the real him. In the corridor, she slows down to let someone walk past, Mikha so close he can smell the conditioner on her hair, feel the warmth rise from her jumper. His heart beats faster, the inside of his abdomen starts to cramp and contort, the white shape knocks at the back of his throat. He clenches his jaw.

He follows Katie through the kitchen and into the back garden. When she opens the glass door, the night wind is cold on his skin. He breathes big gulps to fill his lungs, swallowing air like a man drowning. He sits on a white garden chair to still himself. The ground is muddy, the chair sinks a little. Next to him, Katie sits down too. She wears woollen gloves. Mikha remembers her saying that she doesn't do well in the cold. Always wearing layers, a scarf, a hat.

'I'm Mikha by the way,' he says, offering his hand. He does his best to quiet down his heart, the shaking.

'Katie.'

'Are you cold?'

'What?'

'Cold. Are you cold? It's pretty cold out here...'

She shrugs. 'It's not so bad.'

At the base of Mikha's skull, small beads of sweat make their way down his spine. The white shape swells inside him, scraping the insides of his ribs. Katie takes her phone out from her pocket. The white glow of the screen lights up her face, a beauty spot on her chin. Mikha cannot see what she writes.

'Do you know many people here?' He asks.

'Sorry?'

'This party. Do you know many people here?'

'Not really. It's my brother's birthday.'

She types something on her phone. Her thumb presses on the screen. The buzzing in Mikha's pocket makes him jump, but Katie doesn't see. Doesn't care. He leaves it for a few seconds, enough not to look suspicious. He opens the text.

Hey, so I'm in London
At my brother's party but I
don't know anyone here.
I would still like to see you...?

The January cold seeps into his jumper. He puts the phone away.

'I heard what you said about octopuses,' he ventures. 'You're right, they're smart.'

Katie semi-looks up from her phone. 'Yeah. Guess they are.'

'Do you like animals?'

She winces. 'That's an odd question. Doesn't everyone like animals?'

'I don't know. Maybe not.'

Katie looks at him again.

'Do *you* like animals?' She sneers. The tone of her voice is cutting. It doesn't suit her. Mikha ignores it.

'I do,' he replies, focusing on the mud on his shoes. 'I don't have any pets, but I was thinking of getting one. A rabbit, maybe,' he lies. 'Like, a really big one.'

'Are you serious?' Her face lights up. 'I have a rabbit! But everyone thinks it's weird...'

'I don't think that's weird.' Mikha smiles. He sits back in his chair. 'Rabbits are cute.'

'They are! For Christmas,' she whispers in a conspiratorial tone, 'I made my rabbit a Santa hat. I made holes for the ears and everything... Hang on,' she adds. 'I think I've got a picture.'

She brings her chair closer to Mikha's. When he leans over to see the screen of her phone, the back of his fingers almost brushes against her thigh, so close he could touch her. The white shape contorts in his stomach, he shoves one hand in his pocket to push it down. Katie shows him the picture. He has seen it before. Still, he smiles. Then she puts her phone away and Mikha asks her where she lives. He lets her tell him about Edinburgh, and about things he already knows. He asks all the right questions, watches the little reflections of the lights from the house dance in her eyes as she tells him about her studies, and her flat, her friends. She talks freely. Earnestly. When she mentions how much she wants to travel,

Milk

Mikha feels so at ease he almost mentions faraway plans to visit his sister in New Zealand, and her baby and her husband, but he stops himself just in time.

'I like travelling too,' he says instead.

'Yeah? Been anywhere fun recently?'

'Sure,' he says. Destination hashtags swirl around his brain. Katie looks at him so intently he picks one at random. 'I went to Paris,' he blurts out. But it doesn't sound exciting enough, so he adds: 'I was there when the church burnt down.'

'The cathedral, you mean? Notre-Dame?'

'Yeah,' Mikha corrects himself. 'Notre-Dame, that's the one.'

'That's crazy! What was it like?'

At first, Mikha stalls. But quickly he finds himself summoning BBC footage from the burning church. Clips from the fire he saw on his phone, so many months ago. Panning aerial shots that he turns into descriptions of Parisians in tears, and thick pillars of smoke and collapsing spires, and Katie listens, listens, hanging on every word.

1 am. A thin rain has started to fall, but neither of them cares. It has been almost an hour and Katie hasn't checked her phone once. He recognises her better now, her real-life appearance merges with what she looks like in pictures. When she tells him a joke, Mikha thinks that he could just extend his arm, very simply, and fold a strand of hair behind her ear. There was this one image she sent, late at night, about a week ago. Wearing only trousers and a bra, leaning back on her bed. It superimposes on the real-life Katie and Mikha feels so close to her, for one second, he stops talking. He looks at her and she smiles, but when she leans closer to him, extending one finger so that it almost strokes the back of his hand, the white shape lurches against his throat. Mikha jerks back, wrapping one arm around his body.

'Sorry,' he mumbles through his teeth. 'Sometimes I just get this ache... I'm fine, though' he adds, though his mouth is filling with saliva and he can feel himself starting to retch.

'Are you sure?' She places one hand on his shoulder. Mikha's hair rises on his arm. 'You look... a bit sick, do you feel sick? Do you want water or anything?'

Mikha shakes his head, but his face feels hot, burning.

'Actually yeah, water would be great. Please.'

'Hold on,' she says. 'I'll be back in a sec.'

The rain falls harder now, the grass completely turning to mud. Katie runs into the house and Mikha bends over on his chair, his head hanging between his knees. He shoves his fists into his eye sockets, tries to slow down his breathing but the sickness rises, rises, he feels it crawl and slide. He lifts his coat, looks down. The white shape is showing through the skin. Curling, curling. Another wave coming. Mikha feels his stomach contract. He wills the shape to stay put. Not now, please. Not here. But his muscles do not listen. His body wants to be sick, wants to expel the thing, once and for all. The shape burns through his throat. For a moment, everything around him goes dark. Then he opens his mouth.

When something comes out, it doesn't look like the head.

It is thin and pointy, and white, almost see-through. It slides past the threshold of Mikha's teeth and dangles over his lips. Mikha tries to touch it. It wriggles its way back in. His abdomen contracts. The shape comes out again, longer, and longer, wide like a little finger. Mikha grabs it, the flesh soft as pickled fish. The shape tries to slide back into his throat, he pulls harder. The thing unravels like narrow white ribbon, so long it curls around his hands, his fingers.

It falls into the mud and at first it lies still. But then it uncurls, rubbing its rings together like a sleepy snake.

Behind him, Mikha hears the sound of the garden door.

'Here,' Katie runs over. 'Drink this.'

Mikha doesn't move. Down on the ground, the shape is looking at him. It is covered in mud now, the colour of frog. The head, flat and oblong, two great big black eyes shining like glass beads, and the deep lateral cuts of the gills. Mikha lurches towards it, reaching for its flesh. The skin slides through his fingers.

'What are you doing?' Katie shrieks. She comes closer, looks down. 'Is it... a slug? I hate those things, they're disgusting.' She takes a step forward, lifts one foot. It lands on the shape.

'No!' Mikha screams.

The shape twitches. For a moment it looks dead. Then it burrows down. It digs, disappears into the soil. Mikha plunges both hands in the wet grass, flattening the blades, eyes scanning through mud so dense it looks alive. His fingers uncover snails and earthworms, regular slugs but the shape is nowhere to be seen.

'You scared it!' He shouts, clawing at the earth.

'I did what?'

He runs his fingers through the ground, his hands coated in muck, looking for the shape, but the shape is gone. From a distance, Mikha can hear the faint, regular, almost indistinct bellowing of the train tracks. When he looks up again, Katie stares at him, his wet trousers, his dirty hands. Here and there on the ground, slugs and snails crawl their way to somewhere. Katie frowns and her lips are parted, showing the teeth like people do when they step on spiders.

'It was just a slug,' she says. 'What's wrong with you.'

She still holds the glass of water. Most of it has spilled but she holds on to the glass, presses it to her chest like it's an animal, a creature, something to be protected from him or from the cold of the night.

Katie shakes her head. 'Fucking gross.'

She looks ugly now, Mikha thinks. Ugly and mean.

DAVID ALEXANDER McFARLAND

Loving Sam

What you remember gives pain or pleasure, and mostly I remember being happy when Momma and I settled in Morganville for a time, a good deal longer than most places we stopped. Those were the years when we still were driving around in that Ford, which was looking a bit weary by then, but it still ran pretty well. Momma kept it up as best she could, was always fussy about the interior, and she spent whatever she had to for the engine. *He's the man of the family,* she said to me hundreds of times, *doing the heavy work for us, keeping us going.* She called the car Sam. *Sam needs a new belt,* or *Sam's running hot today, Sam's just got to have new rings,* and she always smiled when she said it, letting her voice ride high. *Sam'll get us there.* But if Sam needed new rings, we ate beans and rice or pancakes for days and skimped on meat and sometimes missed out on breakfast to give Sam what he needed. Everyone, even if they did not know her, even if we had only been in town for a week, let Momma make payments. Sometimes we stayed in a town only long enough to finish out the payments and off we went. *We're moving,* Momma would say, and in an hour we were gone without fuss, without regret, without much emotion about where we had been because Momma was already talking about the next town she had picked out on a map, what we might do there, the friends I could make with boys my age, how she could get a job that lasted more than a month or two. One summer we must have moved three times. Details sometimes grow hazy, and there are just a handful of photographs from those years, mostly Momma with different people, sometimes in back yards, sometimes in a house I do not remember, sometimes in front of stores she must have worked in for a while. Momma never owned a camera that I remember, so these must have been given to her by the people she worked for or by the temporary friends she made, but she kept them carefully. But I do remember a succession of men and a few women telling me how much they loved Momma, but it was never that kind of love that might keep us in a place for long enough for me to make friends that might last.

In Morganville good things seemed to fall into our laps. Momma got a job the first day, a good job she said, and when the fall came, I made a friend or two among the boys at school. The summer persisted long into

September, and I found out when the other boys did that I was pretty good at hitting a baseball. I got picked for games when we divided up, got to be captain a couple of times, and we moved after the first month but only across town to a place lots nicer than I could remember.

'We're staying,' Momma said.

'For how long?'

'For a while, it seems.'

'Things that good?'

'Yessir.' Her way of running words together and letting her voice rise a bit at the end, flapping her hand at the wrist at the same instant she smiled, let me know that everything was as right as it could be. Sam was cooperating, the job bought us new clothes, and Momma had new friends who came by to get her while I was studying math and English and thinking that if we could stay long enough she might let me get a dog. A cat, at the least. This was the year I made friends, and I suppose I was smart enough to begin to realize what it would mean to leave here, to lose friends, to miss someplace. I never missed those other towns and did not miss Momma when she went out, even though there was more of that here than anywhere else we had stopped for a month or more, but she was making friends, too, she said, good friends who were helping us out.

'Aren't we living in a swell place?'

'Yes, ma'am.'

'Aren't we eating pretty good?'

'Yes, ma'am.'

'You've got friends and so do I. We can't complain, can we?'

'No, ma'am.'

'Then let's enjoy ourselves a little bit.' She smiled at me and kissed my cheek. 'I'm proud that you've got some little friends and doing ok in school. We're both doing well.' This was perhaps Momma at her most radiant. Wearing a new dress, her black purse over her arm and holding white gloves, she looked better than any of the mothers of my friends.

In another moment a car horn sounded and she kissed me. 'Do your homework now, Matthew, and get to sleep.'

'Yes, ma'am.'

'I'll look in on you when I get home.'

'All right, Momma.'

'I love you, Baby.'

'Momma, I'm no baby!'

'All right. I love you, *Matthew.*'

'I love you, Momma.' A hurried hug, and she was gone. Our routine—ritual, really. And like all rituals it reassured me then, and in memory comforts me still. But I was not lonely. We were 'self-sufficient,' Momma's words, and we would get through in spite of everything and everyone. *We're tough together, we are. You and me and Sam, we've always survived,* and I believed her. What can a boy do but believe when everything always goes the way your mother says, and she seemed full of knowledge about the world and people and just how everything worked. She had never failed me.

Autumn that year sneaked in while the temperatures were still hot, and winter suddenly sneaked in, too, one substituting one for the other in such a quiet way that hardly anyone noticed until one day people started talking about how far we were along in the season and they seemingly had not noticed until that very day. Baseball was over. The boys I hung out with and I wandered through town in the cold, and I suppose just through our conversations they were beginning to transform me into someone who at the least could understand what living in one place meant—one, two, three generations in one house and no desire to get up and go, expecting and believing that this town, this place was where one could grow up, marry, have children and die happy while not having seen much more than was just in this one spot. This, I now understand, is how they grew up, through conversation and interaction with each other as much as with their parents; surely they were spouting to each other and to me what they had heard at home, but these ideas and attitudes came new to me, such as home ownership.

'Everyone ought to own their own house,' one said.

'We're buying a house next year,' another said.

'You said that last year.'

'You know my dad was out of work. It takes a long time to save up.'

'How much do you need?' I said.

'Hundreds and *hundreds*,' came the answer, 'maybe one or two thousand.' Clearly an impossible-to-conceive-of number. What did any of us know of money and real estate and saving, since we might have had an allowance of a dollar a week. Momma gave me money whenever I asked for it, a dollar or two at a time, never very much, but she always said to spend it carefully. *You never know* accompanied every dollar that passed from her hand to mine.

So far as I knew, Momma and I never saved anything. My mother never said anything about savings, that we had some or that we were doing that. We were living better than ever before here, but I seriously doubted we were saving.

'So, when are you getting a house?' Everyone was looking at me.

'Two years,' I lied. 'Remember, we're still new here, getting settled.'

We were always *getting settled*, and after a few months in Morganville I was seeing a new horizon, beginning to become more independent with Momma working and coming home at seven or eight. We were not so together so much, and she was depending on me now to do some of the cooking, my part of the laundry, to sort the mail into the small pile for her to deal with and the rest for me to goggle at the promises made for every kind of thing people were being asked to buy sight unseen. I knew that was foolish, just as foolish as lying to these boys, because we all knew better—our fate was not in our hands.

So with all the forthrightness that boys can sometimes muster, though dubious of the rightness of my line of thinking, I determined to ask Momma about it. I walked home with my head down, watching my feet take one step after another and then, suddenly, the duplex we had moved into jumped up in front of me before I had figured out any way to ask Momma about a house. Perhaps that was well enough, because there was a Chevy parked beside Sam. Momma was home already, had company, which was a rare thing. She never brought anyone home.

The man could have been invisible for all I knew, because I went running in, flashed by the living room and into her room.

'Whoa, sonny boy, slow down!'

'Whose here?' I nearly shouted out before she could say *Haven't I ever taught you any manners at all?*

'His name is Sam. Sam Waters. Didn't you meet him on the way in? Well, I guess not, since you were in an all-fired hurry. Matthew, go out and introduce yourself. I'll be out in a minute.' She was sitting in front of her dresser, touching up her makeup and waving her hands so her nails would dry.

In retrospect, Sam Waters probably was just an average man of his time, as most men are. Then he appeared too tall for Momma, too brown. What he was wearing I do not remember, but I vividly remember disliking him intensely, instantly when he stood up and stuck out that broad, tanned paw and said, 'Well, you're the Matt I've heard a lot about. I'm Sam.'

No sense of manners, I said to myself because he shortened my name without asking what I like to be called, or was it because he took the lead in a stranger's house. Momma had taught me that men and women who had a refined sense of manners were people we wanted to know, because these were people who thought about living, had sympathy for other people, who were more willing to do favors for people they hardly knew. I had seen it work that way through countless towns. *People without good manners are missing out*, Momma taught. *It's a pleasure to know people who think about themselves and how they fit into the world.*

'Matthew,' I said, trying to be a bit more grownup than I was.

We shook hands and before he let me go, Momma had made her appearance, and Sam was standing, smiling broadly.

'Do I look all right?'

'As right as rain on a hot July day,' Sam said.

'You look fine, Momma,' and she did, a blue dress that matched her eyes fairly closely, high heels, her hair brushed and sprayed down until she had achieved, I could recognize at a glance, her high standard of beauty. I suppose it was no more nor less than the style of the time, but she seemed—no, *was* as beautiful as ever and more, certainly, than the mothers of my friends, more than any woman I knew except the ones on the covers of the magazines she brought home occasionally. They were beautiful by default, by virtue of being on the covers. Momma always said she wished she could be so beautiful.

'Say it, Matthew.'

'*Beau*-ti-ful.' I had to put a little stress on the word. Only old habit saved me here. This was our ritual, and Sam was there; his presence alone interfered in it, cheapened, debased us. For the first time ever I was embarrassed at doing this.

She kissed me as always, leaving a little lipstick that in a moment I would scrub off. 'Be good, Matthew, because you know I'm trusting you. Do your homework and get to bed.'

'No homework.' It was only a small lie.

'Then read something. There's always school stuff you should be reading.'

'All right.'

'I'm going to be late, honey.'

'All right.'

'Good night, Matt.' This from Sam, tall, looming over me like some predatory bird, a hawk, say, measuring me.

'Night.'

With a whirl of her skirts, they were out the door, gone, vanished into Sam's Chevy and headed out for some unknown evening.

I ate something out of the fridge, or I opened a can of something or other. Something or other could be the description of most meals during my childhood; probably a person only remembers a few childhood meals—spectacular feasts at a grandparent's, some restaurant far outside the normal range of eateries usually patronized, or an elaborate meal gone spectacularly wrong or missed entirely by some important, especially invited person. I could have eaten corn beef hash or just a can of corn, slices of bread with butter, some lunch meat. I remember eating, but that is all.

Then, whether minutes or hours later, I was sitting in Sam wrapped up in my coat and the blanket from my bed, listening to the radio, picking up Nashville and Atlanta, Chicago and St. Louis on the dial, and the local stations, Huntsville and Gasden, Arab; the big cities played hot, wild music, and the local stations played mostly country, Hank Williams, Porter Wagoner, Carl Smith, maybe a little Johnnie Cash. Either way, the music was always about love and drinking and the rest sat in the back of my brain, and I turned the dial time after time, resetting the six buttons a couple of times each when the clear channel stations drifted off into static; I knew Momma would be annoyed that I had done that, but the temptation overcame easily the little resistance I put up, because the radio made me think about the nights Momma and I had driven through, the rocking of the car, the warmth of the heater or the air blowing through in the summer while Momma sometimes sang with the radio, saying to a song more than to me, *That's right, baby, that's right*; sometimes I rode with my head in her lap as she drove and talked and sang while I fell in and out of sleep until this was the whole of our life, the incessant swaying and bumping and sleep and light and heat until some town was big enough, busy enough to take us in and let us live there a while before heading out again in what I believed a purely random direction.

And of course this is where they found me, sleeping in the front seat while Sam's music played on weakly at three in the morning, pulled me out while Sam took me in the house and Momma moaning all the time, 'Sam won't start, I just know it. He's dead! I don't have no cables. Who knows if the battery's ruined?' Sam just laughed, put me down on the bed, and pulled my coat off, then pushed me down and tucked my blanket around me.

'I'll get it going,' Sam said.

'Get going, Sam,' I dimly remember saying, and now I cannot be very sure of what I meant. He laughed. And his doing that made Momma mad, I guess, because she started weakly beating at him with her fists—she could never really hurt him—and then I was asleep again.

In the morning he was there. Whether he had gone home and changed clothes or was wearing the same things, I could not say. He was drinking coffee and reading the newspaper, which we never bothered with, at our kitchen table. Momma was out somewhere, maybe working or shopping, or she could have so mad at me that she felt it was better to be someplace else until she could face me and be pretty much as she always was. She never liked to be mad in front of me. *Bad example. It's my job to teach you to behave properly, with other people and with yourself.*

'Coffee, Matt?'

'No. Momma doesn't let me have it.' I said it flatly, as though I was asked that question at least once a week, and plenty of waitresses had made that joke with me in late night coffee shops and diners. I knew the best way to handle that was to confront it head-on.

'You're a tough kid. Your momma's made you into a tough kid.'

What could I do with that? My idea then of a tough kid was one who was willing to fight, a big guy who could knock down anybody his size and lots bigger kids. I was too small, with no muscles, no attitude of restrained violence looking for some alley or playground.

'I've got to get going. Told Sarah that I'd stay till you got up, let you know she's not mad at you. I'll be back in the afternoon. You and I'll get that car moving again.'

'Sam.'

'Yes?'

'The car's name is Sam.'

'Oh.' His lips threatened a smile. 'My mother calls her car Crazy Woman. Like an Indian name. 'Crazy Woman's going to throw us all in a ditch if you three don't settle down!' She loves that old car. Maybe more than she loves us.'

'Momma loves Sam.'

'I hope she does.'

Sam swirled his coat around his shoulder, slipped into it, and was gone before I hardly registered the door closing behind him. My attention had been captured by the easy way he had of talking to me, as easy as I had with the boys I went around with, not like the other men I encountered sometimes who thought they had to win me to get next to Momma.

It was Saturday, and Momma was home by six o'clock; there was no business to be had in Morganville after five because everybody went home by dark to watch whatever they watched on television. We had a radio, we always let it play while we read books, magazines, comic books, whatever had captured our interest lately; this was the year I discovered I liked science, though I suffered some confusion about science and science fiction. By six o'clock Sam and I had pushed big, heavy Sam down the street fast enough for me to pop the clutch and hear it roar into life. I laughed out loud when Sam lurched, coughed, and spun into life. I laughed loudly, because Sam had trusted me and everything had worked. Sam was grinning when he came to take over; we rode around for a while like friends who did not need much talk between them, just the companionability of a shared happiness. When he parked in front of our house, he said, 'That'll take the edge off your momma.'

'Thanks.'

'She loves you, Matthew, but she still has to be your momma.'

'Yeah.' Though I wondered just then if she loved that car more than she loved me.

Momma said, 'Matthew, I'm not mad at you, you know that. I'm deeply disappointed in you, though. You know about running the radio too long, don't you?' I nodded, because I could not trust words right now. 'And we have a perfectly good radio in the house.' She was thinking out loud, just as she always did, sizing up all the factors in her equation—and parents' equations always have more factors than children's—and her calculus produced one answer instantly, without strain over how many decimal points to move and was the answer plus or minus a bit: 'You were mad at me.' She sat down. 'Oh. I had not considered that.'

'No, Momma.'

'He told me you helped him get Sam going.'

'Yeah.'

'He said you and he were all right.'

'We're all right.'

'Maybe everything's not so bad after all.'

'We're all right, Momma.'

'All right, then.' And that was the last talk of it.

In the spring Momma and Sam Norton were married in a small, quick ceremony that did not make the society page of our weekly paper, *The Clarion,* except for a line on page six in the space where all birth and deaths and marriages were listed straight from the county records, and we moved into his house, which was larger; there was an empty bedroom between mine and theirs. We had enough stuff that it took us two trips in Sam to get it all, and my step-dad was not allowed to help us. 'It's always been like this for us,' she told him. And I told all my friends in school that I had a house now, and it seemed that I was just like one of them.

Momma was happy, even though she put on a little weight and had to let out all her dresses. She cooked more, and Sam sometimes cooked burgers and hot dogs on the grill with me. When he realized that I had never really been out in the woods, we went out with a .22 and knocked down a couple of squirrels and field dressed them while he talked a lot about hunting with his dad when he was my age, the first time he got a deer, how he would take Momma and me out fishing on the lake in the spring—which swelled out into a bass fishing trip out on the Tennessee at Gasden. 'Great bass fishing there, best for three hundred miles.'

'Ok,' I said, ready to go right then.

'We'll go next spring,' he promised, and I believed him.

It was difficult not to believe him because he was so earnest about it, and I wanted too much to learn whatever he showed me, hunting, fishing, cars, how to deal with rough boys at school and a small bit about girls, though he said I had a while before all that. And in the early spring—before we had gotten fishing poles for Momma and I and the three of us driven to Gasden—when the drunk driver smashed into his door and pushed his car into a building, it seemed impossible that he and I had not done half the things he talked about, inconceivable that he would never again put his arm around my shoulders and make Momma furious with laughter at the two of us.

I cried openly at the funeral in front of the few people who came to the service, men he worked with, whose wives hugged Momma, and the men shook hands with me. His mother and two sisters were alone on the opposite side of the aisle; Momma tried to talk to them, tried to be as nice as she could, but they walked off, three pale women in black who looked like cartoon mourners. Sam had hardly mentioned them in my hearing, though apparently Momma knew all about them. Aside from the five of us, hardly anyone came to the graveside; Momma tried again with them, but they walked off while she was still speaking.

The first week of May they sent the sheriff out to say we had to the end of the month to move, that it was their house and Momma had no claim on it. Apparently Sam had not changed his will—or his mother had actually owned the house: it was one or the other, but they made Momma cry for days again.

Momma had stopped working a few months before, but now she was out of the house all the time, downtown most of the day while I was in school; I recognized the signs of us moving because she stopped the paper, paid off anybody she owed money to, made sure to fill up Sam's gas tank every other day. She winnowed our wardrobe to the essentials, two pairs of good shoes for me—one brown, one black, five for her—which was one more than she had allowed before. I had a week's worth of clothes that still fit and a suitcase of Sam's that would hold all I had. I had two ties this time. Though I had never paid attention much in the past, each step this time made me want to run away. My friends had drifted away after Sam died, or if they were kept away by their folks, I just do not know. But I was stupendously lonely for the first time, so lonely at a vulnerable age, but every person is at every age vulnerable to a great loss and terrific disappointment and awful loneliness. So, after school was over every day, I lay on my bed and looked at books without reading them, had the radio on without hearing it while I worked through the math of memory to discover the date of our moving.

What threw off my calculations was that she got rid of Sam. The faithful green Ford was gone one day when she unexpectedly picked me up at school in the red Chevy, Sam's car. I thought his mother had taken it.

'No, Matthew. I was just having it checked over. You know how Sam kept this car up good.'

'Yes, ma'am.'

'This is Sam, now.'

'Oh.' Sam was red, a Chevy, a bigger car that carried a new set of jumper cables and a small set of tools. It was clean inside and out. 'He's the heavy lifter for us now,' which told me we were leaving tomorrow, a week ahead of school letting out. But those niceties had never bothered us before. 'He'll get us through. Sam's never failed me.' She spoke with that satisfaction and energy that approached earlier days.

But I was wrong. Momma seemed somehow reluctant to go, so I did finish school that year; the very next morning we left at six in the morning, taking all the back roads to the state highway that runs south to Birmingham, north to Nashville. We turned south and so far as I know, neither of us has been in Morganville since.

A week ago I had a letter from them, Momma and Sam. Oh, his color and shape has changed a lot over the years; every two or three months a card or letter comes, and since I'm always in Atlanta, have lived in this big, rambling house for so awfully long, everything reaches me. I write back immediately, and maybe one reply out of three reaches them. Momma wrote this time, *We're so tired, Matthew, Sam and I. Our rings are going, and we can't do what we used to. We're shabby, both of us, bad clothes and tired paint. But the sun still looks good out over the water in the mornings and the evenings. I don't know which is better.*

RACHEL SLOAN

The Judgment of Paris

It's one of those June days you only get here – the first of the year, in fact – and in an ideal world you'd be on the terrace of that café near the Pont de la Tournelle, the one just far enough east to escape the plague of tourists, with a pastis in front of you, no more essays to mark, nothing to weigh on your conscience, nothing to do but watch the kaleidoscope of leaf shadows and passersby.

But nobody ever said it was an ideal world, and instead you're at the Louvre on your first blind date, post-breakup.

You've chosen the Roman galleries partly as a nod to his interest in classical history, mostly out of expediency (unlikely to be rammed on a Saturday afternoon) and you're repenting it. They've always bored you stiff. There's no chance of losing yourself amid this white forest of numbingly identical bodies. No chance of forgetting who you're with, and why.

You found him through a dating website aimed at expats. On paper – on screen, rather – he sounded mildly promising: a British lawyer, recently posted to his firm's Paris office. He seemed friendly, polite, inoffensively amusing in the few messages you exchanged. His photos gave you pause, but you reminded yourself that Julien never photographed well, that his beauty lay in the mobility of his features and the camera always coarsened his face beyond repair. You showed them to several friends, who were divided: some said *brave girl, putting yourself out there*, others hemmed and hawed, *don't you think it's a bit soon?* You had a massive argument with your mother, who'd treasured the hope that now that you and Julien are through you'd give up this ten-year Paris malarkey and come home, and didn't take kindly to you pointing out the minor detail of your career. If nothing else, it's experience, you told yourself. Whether it's good remains to be seen.

It's practically summer so you've dressed for it. A blue-and-white striped sundress, sling-back espadrilles. No makeup, partly because you can still get away without it and partly because you can't be bothered. You started to regret it the moment you joined the ticket queue. You feel raw. Peeled. It would have been nice to have some sort of armour.

Your heart sank the moment you saw him standing under the lightwell of the pyramid, that slight bespectacled figure in chinos and a linen jacket.

The photos hadn't lied. Or rather, they had. They hadn't shown you how weak his chin was, or what a pale, watery grey his eyes were. There's something about his smile that makes your skin prickle, though you can't put your finger on what. It's bland, amiable, ingratiating. There's nothing discernibly off about it, and yet... You hope your disappointment doesn't show.

Your conversation as you ramble among the gods and warriors isn't terrible, you suppose. He isn't uninteresting. You have enough in common for it never to sputter to a complete, mortifying halt. You wonder if this is how a first-date conversation is supposed to go, if you and he are playing your parts quite right. You're more than ten years out of practice. You feel like a shucked oyster. *Please scrape me off the plate and put me back in my shell.* He's unfailingly solicitous – ushering you through doors, fingertips lightly pressing the back of your elbow, constantly checking on you, deferring to your every opinion – and it occurs to you that this is what unsettles you more than his looks. You're not used to being treated like a piece of porcelain. *Stop comparing him to Julien*, you remind yourself. Under the polite artifice of it all you're already wondering how to let him down gently at the end of it. Whenever that happens.

He suggests tea and you dare to hope that it might mean an escape from this marble tomb but it turns out he means the salon de thé overlooking the pyramid. He insists you take the banquette and the tea is shockingly overpriced and the lemon tartlet sickly sweet, but then he asks about your work and he seems genuinely interested when you start telling him about teaching comparative literature at the American University. You tell him about how you recently took your students to see a production of Gombrowicz's *Ivona, Princess of Burgundy* at one of the little experimental theatres in the Bois de Vincennes and what an impression it made on them, and you. He doesn't know the play so you describe it.

'It's set in this corrupt, glittering, decadent court where the prince, in a moment of madness, decides to marry a mute, ugly, gauche peasant girl. And the moment he brings her into the court she causes chaos. Simply by sitting there and saying nothing she's a rebuke to the artificiality and the rottenness of the place. She's like a mirror in which everyone sees themselves properly for the first time, and it drives them over the edge. So naturally, they kill her.'

'And everything returns to normal?'

'No. They think it will, but they soon see that normal no longer exists. All they can ever do is pretend it does.'

'Prisoners in a cage of their own devising, eh?' There's a spark in his eye, a shift in his voice that makes you realise you got him wrong. He *understands.* He gets it, from which it's only a step to he gets *you.* Suddenly you're thinking that this afternoon hasn't been a waste after all. You're still going to have to find some way to politely tell him you're not interested in him *that* way, but you may have gained a friend. Now you're imagining meeting up with him some future afternoon or evening to talk books over a pastis at that place near the Pont de la Tournelle and you relax into your dress, into the banquette, the afternoon.

When he asks if you fancy another round of the galleries you now feel comfortable offering to show him one of your favourites and you set off together, letting yourself luxuriate in this vague new complicity, your espadrilles whispering over the marble floors.

If a fire broke out in the Louvre and you could only save one room, you wouldn't hesitate a second: the Watteaus, every time. You feel unaccountably anxious leading him into their midst. In a way, it's like introducing him to your friends. Only they can't defend themselves and they can't pass judgment of their own.

Melancholy Gilles, dignified in the puffs of his silvery suit, alone in the midst of a mugging crowd. The frozen pavane of the pilgrims forever embarking for, or from, Cythera. The mysterious crowd in rustling silks milling around a twilit pond, the ladies' napes set aglow by the rising moon. Hello, hello, old friends.

In the vitrine of smaller pictures is your guilty favourite. You know it's far from his best painting but you've always felt an absurd affection for *The Judgment of Paris*, precisely because it thumbs its nose so blithely at the chilly perfection of the Greeks and Romans. Because Venus, with her spindly legs and blonde bilboquet head and generous, dimpled buttocks, doffing her chemise for a Paris who looks like a schoolboy who's gotten into the cider and is trying to look cool and failing miserably, is imperfect and ludicrous and *human.* 'Here, come and look at this one,' you gesture him over in that half-whisper that galleries and libraries impose.

'Mmm,' he hums, gazing at it over the top of his glasses. 'I imagine she's asking him *does my arse look big in this.'*

For a second you can't believe your ears. You steal a glance at him but he doesn't look mortified or as if he's expecting you to share the joke or even much aware of your presence at all, and your disbelief gives way to rage. (Rage and also obscure hurt on Venus's account, because she can't turn around and give him the finger, or fry him to a crisp or make him fall in love with a newt.) You want to ask him in what universe he thinks it's acceptable to say that to a woman he's just met. Why he thinks that playing the perfect gentleman entitles him to utter horrors like that. Whether he actually expected you to find it witty and amusing.

But you can't. You can't say a thing. Your tongue's frozen. You've spent your whole life being nice. Being polite. Turning the other cheek. Your politesse has grown over your mouth like tree bark and you're trapped inside. Any second now you're going to bleat out a shamefaced laugh and shrug it off, act as if nothing happened (besides, maybe you deserve it, for being fool enough to believe he might have been a kindred spirit) –

Your phone pings.

You scrabble madly for it while trying to appear not to. It's only an automated message offering you fifty free minutes at weekends for the next three months but suddenly you love France Telecom and are ready to award it the Légion d'Honneur for services to humanity. You shove the phone back in your bag and glance wildly at him, composing your face into a careful mask of panic.

'Oh gosh, I can't believe it,' you gasp. 'I completely forgot I'd promised my friend Nadège I'd pick her daughter up from her violin lesson this afternoon.' (There are no Nadèges in your circle of acquaintance, you've just always liked the name.) 'I'm really sorry, I've got to dash, what bad luck, *so* sorry to cut short a lovely afternoon...' You find yourself giving into the unaccustomed pleasure of this aria of lies, any guilt at deceiving him tamped down with *he damned well deserves it*, any anger at your own cowardice (which will keep you awake for nights afterward) temporarily cancelled by the thrill of your impending escape.

'Oh, not at all, it's just unfortunate. I hope we can make up for it another time,' he says, bland and unruffled, and you say a hurried goodbye and – prisoner of politesse that you are – give him two hurried air kisses and three more fluttering apologies before you tear off, thanking some higher power that you had the presence of mind not to give him your number.

It's not until you're halfway across the Pont des Arts that you slow to your normal pace, heart thudding. The sun's still shining. You turn your face and shoulders up to it, only now aware how cold it was in the Louvre. You've still got most of the afternoon ahead of you. There's a table and a pastis with your name on it at your favourite café (and God, you could do with a drink). When you get to the other side you stop and draw a long, shuddering breath and realise it's the first time you've breathed freely all day.

It will be a long time before you can look at Watteau again.

FLASH FICTION FIRST PRIZE

ROWENA WARWICK

Mum Died

Mum died reaching for a packet on the top shelf of a kitchen cupboard. She died cleaning out the rabbit hutch, and again after a dog ate Hazel. I was sitting on the back-doorstep shelling peas when it happened. Somehow, I wasn't surprised. She died again when her car ran into a stationary vehicle, you remember? We were on the way home from ballet in Harlow, that man shouted but it didn't matter because mum was dead. She died in the pub while we were sitting outside with our crisps and once more singing at church, where there was a pillar and we couldn't see her. Before all this she had died several times in Dad's Ford Anglia when he was teaching her to drive, luckily it was only her. Later she died when I got my A level results, a grand death with histrionics and proper flowers. She died in those shoes which were the wrong colour on my wedding day and frequently since in the photos. She died with the arrival of each grandchild, there have been six, or perhaps she was already dead having suffered through each delivery. She died magnificently when she retired and again at the bungalow, such a lovely garden, the pond, the tree heavy with plums. But more recently she has used it all up, her skill in dying. Thin as a wisp she lies, grasping the covers as if she might fall, as if death might not be able to catch her.

FLASH FICTION SECOND PRIZE

GAYNOR JONES

Tamed

He's pushing my head down, down, but tonight I'm resisting; not because I don't want to, but because I want to stay. Here. Here where his mouth next to mine breathes salt-smoke and beer. Here where his tongue is inside me. Searching me. Feeling me. Wanting me.

I push my body onto his and he moans and the sound is wet and his tongue is wet and I am wet. It's all slow and fast and real and not real and I hear the others, behind the door, as they keep watch, or try to see, or wait their turn.

And years later when *I* am older, and *I* am in control, and *I* am powerful, I tell a group of girls while they sit bored, folding paper, shifting in their seats,

'You can say stop anytime you want.'

And

'Your body can't tell the difference between fear and excitement.'

(Ain't that the truth?)

And I remember how he closed the bedroom door and I remember how I'd told him 'I never do anything wild.'

And how it would be my wild story to tell of my wild thing. But what I didn't realise, because I was too young to realise, was that I would be silenced while people told that wild story about me and him, but mostly about me.

And that the story would follow me around for years, like the taste of his tongue in my mouth, or the bruises on my breasts in the days after.

FLASH FICTION THIRD PRIZE

OLGA MORONI

Fabulous at Fifty

You stick out like a sore thumb and they know the Latin rite. Sex is fucked up. You are, or at least, were, in the past, a Catholic. Your husband provides for you. And they know this from your olive skin, hair severely slicked back into a pony tail. They know this because you bow your head slightly, when asked to do anything, as if you were a lapsed Japanese. They know this because you never do anything exciting at the weekend to talk about. So when they ask you if you believe in life after death you tell them 'Yes. I am dead already and in more than one way. I have no children, no high earning job to be independent by. I left what I knew behind. No one is more surprised than myself that I keep on living'. Expecting only a *yes*, they were unprepared for your verbal aggression. You took the bait and threw it back. 'You've left the fridge door open' you say. Their mouths draw a helpless 'Oh' as their green credentials are momentarily lost. Loss of professional virtue is fatal. You have another fire to put out this morning and walk out of the staff room. They sit down on sofas for their early lunch, their manes of shampooed, conditioned and blow-dried hair swaying gently. They indulge in a mindless ritual, teasing out grains of couscous from their lunch boxes, translucent and heaped like rosary beads, with the tines of their dainty forks.

DORSET PRIZE AND YOUNG WRITER AWARD

LYDIA CLARK

Bring and Buy

She never has enough.

At the counter, groceries stack, her child whines.

'No problem,' the kindly owner chirps, 'pay with what you can.' She strips her purse of coppers, pats the pockets of her mac. She unhooks both earrings, slips off her dead husband's ring.

'Perfect,' he smiles. That night, their stomachs dance.

The cupboards bloat with air. Her child removes his shirt and smooths it out, forks invisible steak. At the store, the game continues.

'I'll do you a deal,' the owner grins, feathers plumped, 'your home for three items on my shelves.' She plucks the soap, the pads, the pack of blue socks. For fun, they lay a table, dream of brimming plates.

Her child sleeps too much. Limbs writhe and absent cheeks blow out his father's name. Praying doesn't rouse him. She wraps him in her cardigan, smacks along the pavement.

'Poor thing,' the owner murmurs, 'let me help.'

She takes some butter, bread, a pack of beans. From the arms of his new keeper, her child bleats goodbye.

Without him, there's no trudging forward. She wanders free, but desperation drags her back.

'I've nothing left,' she weeps beneath the owner's wing. He wipes away warm tears, points towards her chest. She rips her breasts apart, reaches in ribs snapping, slaps her beating heart against the counter.

'There,' she shrieks, with velvet running down her wrists.

He extends his neck, beak poised.

The eggs are hers. The milk is hers. She staggers home, neither dead nor living.

NICOLA SHILCOCK

The one about the hole in the front garden

One day it wasn't there, then the next it was. It was the summer holidays, so the days had lost their names and colours. Sunday was no longer grey-blue and weighty. Wednesday was no longer lemony. Saturday had lost its bright green glaze. There were hot days, when we rode bikes and lit fires in grass, and far-too-hot days when all we could do was bob about in water like hippos. The hole was very deep with clean, straight sides – an inverted sandcastle – but somewhere near the bottom was a glimpse of something that shouldn't be seen, like when Owen's sister Amelia got her leg caught under the roundabout – a corner or shard of something sharp that should have stayed covered. 'Something to do with the foundations,' they said as we circled it, unbelieving, sucking on orange ice pops.

RICHARD SMITH

On a Supermarket Toilet Floor

Carol can hear a rattle in her head, but it can't be her own breathing because she's dead, she did it properly this time, no messing with tablets, this time she had a shiny cut-artery razor and a bottle of Grey Goose vodka, and there was no pain, well not much, and the cut was so deep she could have put half her baby's arm in it, if she knew where her baby was, but that's another thing, another piece-of-shit thing adding together with all the other things, like the dad thing, and the shitty boyfriend thing, and now here's another man doing something to her she doesn't want and his badge says Carl,

who almost doesn't know where to start, there's so much blood, it's everywhere, like it was in the desert sometimes, but it's slippery here, not drying into the sand, and this girl can't be twenty yet, then out of nowhere Carl sees Corporal Bell, who bled out and died, and now this girl will die if he doesn't find a vein soon, but Bell-boy didn't have any veins to find, or arms, and Carl is cold sweating even though he has the needle attached to the saline, and then suddenly it's in, and he can get her to the ambulance, this girl

who is shouting at him with her eyes, No this isn't what I want,

and because Carl's seen this before he understands but says, Sorry love it's my job.

Biographies

Judges' biographies

Mimi Khalvati was born in Tehran, Iran and has lived most of her life in London. She has published nine collections with Carcanet Press, including *The Meanest Flower*, shortlisted for the T.S. Eliot Prize 2007, and *Child: New and Selected Poems 1991-2011*, a Poetry Book Society Special Commendation. Her *Very Selected Poems* appeared from Smith/Doorstop in 2017. She has held fellowships at the International Writing Program in Iowa, the American School in London and at the Royal Literary Fund, and her awards include a Cholmondeley Award from the Society of Authors and a major Arts Council Writer's Award. She is the founder of the Poetry School and a Fellow of the Royal Society of Literature and of The English Society. Her new book of sonnets, *Afterwardness*, published by Carcanet in October 2019, is a Poetry Book Society Winter Wild Card.

Nell Leyshon is an award-winning novelist and playwright. Her first novel, *Black Dirt*, was long-listed for the Orange Prize and *The Colour of Milk* has been published worldwide. She won the *Evening Standard* award for best new playwright and was the first woman to write for Shakespeare's Globe. She also writes for radio and her first radio play won the Richard Imison Award. Nell taught creative writing for many years with marginalised communities, and runs The Outsiders Project which makes work for theatre written and performed by outsider artists. She is Deputy Chair of the Shakespeare's Globe.

Writers' biographies

Luke Allan is poetry editor at Partus Press and co-editor of the journals *Pain and Oxford Poetry*. Born in Newcastle, he studied literature and creative writing at UEA and Oxford and is former managing editor at Carcanet Press and *PN Review*. He won the 2019 Charles Causley Prize and placed third in the 2019 Mick Imlah Prize and the 2020 Poets & Players Competition. He is currently working on his debut collection.

Erika Banerji is a writer and journalist. Her stories have been published and listed for awards including the Brick Lane Bookshop, Lorian Hemingway, V. S. Pritchett and London Short Story Prize. In 2019 her story was in the top sixty entries in The BBC NSSA. Erika is on the shortlist for the 2020 Bristol Short Story Prize. She is an alumna of the Faber Academy 'Writing a Novel' Course and the London Library Emerging Writers Program 2019-20. Erika is working on her first novel, set in 1960s Bengal and London. She lives in London. Find her at www.erikabanerji.com

Lydia Clark graduated from Warwick University with a BA in English Literature and Creative Writing in 2018, and an MA in Writing in 2019. Her work has been published or anthologised with Bath Flash Fiction, Ellipsis Zine, Lunate Fiction, National Flash Fiction Day, and Reflex Press. She is currently working on her first novel. Twitter: @Lydia_Clark_

Alistair Daniel is an Associate Lecturer at the Open University, where he is working on a PhD in Creative Writing. His short stories have been published in various journals, including *The Missouri Review*, *The Stinging Fly*, *Narrative*, *Litro*, *The Irish Times* and *Stand*. He has held the Charles Pick Fellowship at the University of East Anglia, and is completing his first novel, *Montreal*, the opening pages of which were shortlisted for the Northern Writers Award in 2018.

Alex Dawes is originally from London but now lives in the East Midlands with his girlfriend and his dog. He studied Political Science at the University of East Anglia but ended up working in financial services. 'The Note' will be his second short story published this year.

Jonathan Edwards has two poetry collections, *My Family and Other Superheroes* and *Gen*, both published by Seren. He has received the Costa Poetry Award and twice been winner of the People's Choice Award at the Wales Book of the Year. He lives in Crosskeys, South Wales, and is Editor of *Poetry Wales*.

John Freeman was born in Essex, grew up in south London, and taught for many years at Cardiff University. His poetry has been widely published in magazines and anthologies and in ten collections, of which the most recent is *What Possessed Me* (Worple Press), which won the poetry section of the Wales Book of the Year competition and the Roland Mathias prize in 2017. In 2018 his poem 'Exhibition' won first prize in the Bridport competition. He lives in a village in the Vale of Glamorgan.

Biographies

Elizabeth Fremantle is the author of *Queen's Gambit, Sisters of Treason, Watch the Lady* and *The Girl in the Glass Tower*. As EC Fremantle she has written *The Poison Bed* and *The Honey and the Sting*, all published by Michael Joseph (Penguin). Her short fiction has been published in MIR and the *Sunday Express*. She is a graduate of the Birkbeck MA in Creative Writing and has contributed journalism to various publications including *Vogue*, *Vanity Fair*, *The Sunday Times*, *The Wall Street Journal* and *The Financial Times*. She lives in London. Her website is Elizabethfremantle.com

Rachael Fulton is a tiny, animal-loving editor living in a small town in South West Scotland. In the course of an eclectic, colourful career she has been a comic book editor (NETFLIX, Millarworld), a TV reporter, a cookery show producer and a digital journalist (STV.) She now spends her days writing stories, running The King's Arms Hotel in Castle Douglas with her family, and exploring the countryside with her dog, Bunny. Rachael is media editor for Glasgow publishing imprint The Common Breath, and hopes to publish more of her own writing this year.

Cara George is a fiction writer. She studied Fine Art at The Ruskin in Oxford and Goldsmithing at the Royal College of Art in London before completing an MA in Creative Writing at University of East Anglia. Cara was longlisted for the National Poetry Competition in 2017 and was awarded The Sir Malcolm Bradbury Memorial Scholarship at UEA in 2019. Cara's darkly comic short stories are about sex as mistranslation and what happens between characters during sensory disarticulation. She is currently writing her first novel, *Homemade*, a granular story about solitude, animal consciousness and the body as trauma.

Karen Green co-edited *Lyrical Ballads* for the Cornell Wordsworth series (1994), attended Laurie Smith's class at the City Lit and had poems published in *Magma* magazine. Later she joined the Magma Board, working in production and editing. She attended classes at the Poetry School and co-edited an Advanced Poetry Workshop publication with Mimi Khalvati (2006). She had various poems placed through competitions. 'Citadel of the Husband' commended in the first Troubadour competition, 'Shirley' commended in the Flamingo Feather competition in 2013. Recently she had two poems in Issue 46 of *Brittle Star*, 'Other People's Wives' and 'Self-Examination'.

Biographies

Sarah Harte won the Bryan MacMahon Short Story award at Listowel Writer's Week in 2019. She has been shortlisted, longlisted and highly commended for prizes both in Ireland and in the UK, including the Bridport Short Story Prize in 2019, The Sean O'Faolain Short Story Prize 2019, The Manchester Fiction Prize in 2017. In 2020 she was longlisted for The Fish Short Story Prize. She's currently finishing her first collection of short stories and is writing a novel. She has previously published two novels with Penguin Ireland.

Justin Hunt grew up in rural Kansas and lives in Charlotte, North Carolina, USA. In 2012, he retired from a long international business career in order to write. His work appears or is forthcoming in *Five Points, Michigan Quarterly Review, New Ohio Review, The Florida Review, Bellingham Review, Southword* (Ireland), *The Strokestown Poetry Anthology* (Ireland), *Live Cannon* (U.K.), *Arts & Letters, The Atlanta Review,* and *Spoon River Poetry Review*, among other journals and publications.

Gaynor Jones is a writer and spoken word performer currently based in Oldham. She has won the Bath Flash Fiction Award and the Mairtín Crawford Short Story Award and was named Northern Writer of the Year at the 2018 Northern Soul Awards. Her short story collection, *Girls Who Get Taken & Other Stories*, won a Northern Debut Award at the 2020 Northern Writers' Awards. She has been published in various literary journals and anthologies and has created bespoke spoken word pieces for local festivals. She performed at the 2019 Edinburgh Fringe with For Books Sake.

Michael Lavers is the author of *After Earth,* published by the University of Tampa Press. His poems have appeared in *Crazyhorse, 32 Poems, The Hudson Review, Best New Poets 2015, TriQuarterly, The Georgia Review,* and elsewhere. He has been awarded the Chad Walsh Poetry Prize and the University of Canberra Vice-Chancellor's International Poetry Prize. Together with his wife, the writer and artist Claire Åkebrand, and their two children, he lives in Provo, Utah, and teaches poetry at Brigham Young University.

Nida Manzoor is a writer/director working in TV. She has most recently directed episodes of Doctor Who and BBC3 series 'Enterprice' winning an Royal Television Society award for comedy directing in 2019. Nida is preparing to shoot her first original show 'Lady Parts' as writer/director for Channel 4 and NBC.

Biographies

Laurane Marchive is a French writer and director living in London. Her stage work, a mixture of immersive theatre and contemporary circus, has won numerous awards, including an Off West End Award. Her writing has appeared in *3am Magazine*, *The London Magazine*, *The Mechanics' Institute Review*, *Review 31* and the *TLS*. She was recently shortlisted for the Spread The Word Life Writing Prize (2019) and the London Short Story Prize (2020). In 2020 she was also Highly Commended in the Spread The Word Life Writing Prize.

David Alexander McFarland was born in Tennessee, raised in Alabama, served in the US military, worked in factories, retail shops, as an insurance salesman, and had many other jobs before finally earning his Master's degree in English, thereafter teaching college English for 33 years. He lives in northwestern Illinois at the only place where the Mississippi River runs east to west. His short stories, essays, and poetry have appeared widely. He found time to keep bees, grow a vegetable garden, and loved being the stay-at-home parent for his two children.

Dafydd Mills Daniel teaches at the University of Oxford and is a BBC Radio 3 New Generation Thinker. He has written short stories since reading Chekhov's 'The Kiss' twenty years ago, but, until now, hasn't been brave enough to submit any of them anywhere! As a university lecturer, he has so far published non-fiction. He is author of *Conscience and the Age of Reason* and *Briefly: 25 Great Philosophers, From Plato to Sartre*. His radio and TV documentaries include: *Sir Isaac Newton and the Philosophers' Stone*, *Where do human rights come from?* and *The Story of God with Morgan Freeman*.

Rowland Molony spent eight years in Rhodesia-Zimbabwe. The involvement with African bushveld and its wildlife resulted in a collection of poems entitled Frogs & Co; these were responses to frogs, chameleons, lizards, snakes, ants, bees, monkeys, spectacular rainstorms and granite wildernesses that predate the presence of humanity on the earth by hundreds of millions of years. He met and married the artist Elizabeth Baxendale in Bulawayo and their two daughters, Emma and Susie, were born in that beautiful city. He retired in 2002 after 30 years of teaching English Literature.

Olga Moroni is originally from Castelo Branco, Portugal, and has lived in Scotland for twenty-two years. She belongs to Mearns Writers, a writing group in Stonehaven. Her poems appeared in their anthologies *Stoney*

Scrievers (2009), *Pens & Palettes* (2010) and *An Excitement of Possibilities* (2012). She is published in *Pushing Out the Boat* (2007). She has worked with children with special needs, as an oil lab technician and library assistant. She has a BA (Honours) in Art History and is volunteer threat detector for the Woodland Trust. Apart from loving art and trees, she enjoys running and completed her first Edinburgh marathon in 2018.

Beverley Nadin was awarded a doctorate in Creative Writing at Newcastle University in 2019. Her work was commended in the 2014 National Poetry Competition, won second prize in the 2014 *Poetry London* Competition, and is published in *PN Review*, *The Rialto*, *The North*, *Magma*, and *Stand*.

John O'Donoghue lives in Brighton and teaches Creative Writing at the Brighton Writers' Centre. His short story 'The Irish Short Story That Never Ends' won The Irish Post Creative Writing Competition in 2016, and in 2019 he co-founded The Wild Geese Press, Books From The Irish Diaspora http://www.thewildgeesepress.com

Mario Petrucci is a poet, ecologist, PhD physicist and Royal Literary Fund Fellow. He has held major poetry residencies at the Imperial War Museum and BBC Radio 3. *Negatives*, written during his time at the museum, won the 1999 Bridport Prize. *Heavy Water: a poem for Chernobyl* (Enitharmon) secured the *Daily Telegraph*/Arvon Prize and 'inflicts... the finest sort of shock, not just to the senses, but to the conscience, to the soul' (*Poetry London*). *i tulips* (Enitharmon) takes its name from his 1111-strong Anglo-American sequence, acclaimed for its innovation and humanity. Petrucci's award-winning translation work includes Montale (Arc) and Hafez (Bloodaxe).

Maya C. Popa is the author of *American Faith* (Sarabande Books), winner of the 2020 North American Book Prize, and two pamphlets, including *The Bees Have Been Canceled*, a PBS Summer Choice in 2017. She is the Poetry Reviews Editor at *Publishers Weekly* and a PhD candidate at Goldsmiths, University of London, writing on the role of wonder in poetry.

Julie-ann Rowell's fourth poetry collection, *Exposure*, was published in September 2019 by Turas Press, Dublin, and is about the Orkney islands. Her first pamphlet *Convergence* (Brodie Press) won a Poetry Book Society Award. Her collection *Letters North* was nominated for the

Michael Murphy Poetry Prize for Best First Collection in Britain and Ireland in 2011. Her pamphlet collection, *Voices in the Garden*, about Joan of Arc, was published by Lapwing Publications, Belfast in 2017. She has been teaching poetry and mentoring for fifteen years and has an MA in Creative Writing from Bath Spa University.

Nicola Shilcock lives and works in North London, currently as a primary school teacher. Before becoming a teacher, she graduated from Central Saint Martins, in Fine Art. She is inspired by, and envious of, children's capacity to start a project with no anxiety about where it will end, be it a story, a game, a piece of engineering or a piece of theatre.

Di Slaney lives in an ancient farmhouse in Nottinghamshire where she runs livestock sanctuary Manor Farm Charitable Trust and independent publisher Candlestick Press. Her poems have been published in *Poetry Wales, Popshot, Magma, The Rialto, The Interpreter's House* and *Brittle Star*, twice shortlisted for the Bridport Prize and Plough Prize, and highly commended in the Forward Prizes. Her first collection *Reward for Winter* was published by Valley Press in 2016 and her second collection *Herd Queen* in September 2020. She is poet in residence at Nottinghamshire Local History Association.

Rachel Sloan is an art historian, curator and writer. Born and raised in Chicago, she has lived in the UK for most of her adult life. She has recently finished writing a novel. 'The Judgment of Paris' is her first published piece of fiction.

Richard Smith is mid-way through a part-time MA in Creative Writing at Keele University, which has allowed him to develop more faith in his writing, and he used this summer to complete his memoir, *Distance*. He has been writing for ten years, and his work has appeared in the *Aesthetica Creative Writing Annual, Henshaw Three* and several flash fiction anthologies. He obtained his first degree as a mature student after some years in the army, and has spent the time since, in a variety of jobs, being currently employed in supermarket retail.

Rowena Warwick writes from her home in Oxfordshire. She has a Diploma in Creative Writing from Oxford University and an MA in Creative Writing from Bath Spa, both with distinction. Her poetry has been listed and placed in a number of competitions and is widely published in magazines. She has been longlisted in the national poetry competition. Her short stories have made the short list of both the Cambridge and Bristol competitions this year. She is currently editing her first novel. When not writing she works in the health service. She tweets at @rowena_warwick

Debra Waters was born and bred in Yorkshire and now lives in South London with her husband and child and works as a lifestyle writer and digital editor. In 2020, she graduated from Goldsmiths with an MA in Creative & Life Writing, where she gained a Distinction. Debra writes short stories, autofiction and flash fiction and has been shortlisted for the Pat Kavanagh Award, longlisted for the London Library Emerging Writers Programme, and published in *Flash Flood*.